51 Bus route

Fox Twine

Robert Robinson found up here

DUMP GANG HQ

boring tennis

Farmer Jenkins (TWAT)

This is
THIS COUNTRY

KERRY + KURTAN
RULE THIS
VILLAGE 4 EVA!

DARREN
LACEY is
GRANNY
BASHING SCUM

This is

THIS COUNTRY

The REAL S*** that goes down in our village.
It ain't just fetes and duck races, you know.

Kerry and Kurtan Mucklowe

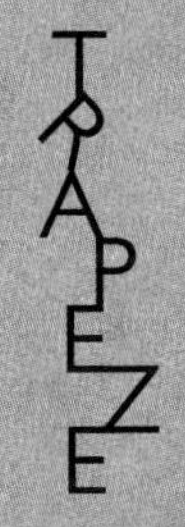

First published in Great Britain in 2019 by Trapeze,
an imprint of The Orion Publishing Group Ltd
Carmelite House, 50 Victoria Embankment,
London EC4Y 0DZ

An Hachette UK company

5 7 9 10 8 6 4

A CIP catalogue record for this book is
available from the British Library.

ISBN (Hardback): 978 1 4091 9111 7
ISBN (ebook): 978 1 4091 9112 4

Designed by Julyan Bayes at us-now.com

Printed in Italy

www.orionbooks.co.uk

Dedication

This book is dedicated to the brother of 13-time Premier League champion and all round legend Ryan Giggs. Can't remember his name but I think he'll be pleased to know that he was mentioned in something, rather than his brother Ryan Giggs who hogs all the limelight. May Ryan Giggs's brother's name [insert here] remain in print for a thousand years.

DUMP
GANG

SLUG
is a
Girlfrind-stealin
NOB

Contents

Welcome to this month's village newsletter! This issue is an exciting one as it has been guest-edited by our very own Kerry and Kurtan Mucklowe, who showed a keen interest in helping out. Other than the odd contribution here and there, it has been lovely to take a break from my usual newsletter responsibilities so I can spend more time in the church and on the golf course! This issue takes a bit of a twist, as we left it up to you villagers to contribute anything of interest about yourself or the village in general. We were overwhelmed with submissions, and a special mention to Kerry and Kurtan, who worked very hard collecting much of the content (with permission, I hope!).

As always, I expect to see lots of examples in this issue of our community working together and supporting one another. This is something that has always been very special about this village, and long may it continue.

Just a quick note to say I'm delighted to bring you news that our very own newsletter distributor, Morris Parker, has received a card from Her Majesty the Queen this month. Congratulations, Morris, on reaching your 100th birthday! If you see him on his bike putting this newsletter through your door, please take the time to wish him happy birthday. Thank you, Morris, for all your hard work. Still pedalling up and down those hills after all these years – you're an inspiration to us all.

And, while we're on the subject of newsletter distribution, I do get people contacting me now and again to say that the month has passed before they receive their newsletter. I would like to remind everyone that the newsletter is written and distributed entirely by volunteers and that we all do our very best to get your edition to you as soon as possible, come rain or shine!

Yours faithfully,

Francis Seaton

Reverend Francis Seaton

LONSDALE

KERRY AND KURTAN'S 'GETTING BACK ON TRACK' CONTRACT

C:\Users\rev.francis\documents\contracts\kerryandkurtan.doc

CONTRACT

I, Kerry Mucklowe/Kurtan Mucklowe (circle as appropriate), hereby promise the Vicar, Reverend Francis Charles Seaton, that I WILL:

1. Actively look for employment, which includes: typing up a CV with Reverend Francis Seaton; applying for jobs online; enquiring around the village; and spending time practising interview techniques, for at least 1 hour a week with Reverend Francis Seaton.
2. Promise to have a positive attitude and outlook.
3. Promise to take editing the village newsletter seriously, and not to use it as a tool to upset or offend.
4. Promise to be courteous to those who live in the village.
5. Promise to be courteous to those who are visiting the village.
6. Promise to channel my energy into only positive tasks.
7. Promise to believe in my potential and ability – and not to give up!

I, Kerry Mucklowe/Kurtan Mucklowe (circle as appropriate), hereby promise the Vicar, Reverend Francis Charles Seaton, that I WILL NOT:

1. Loiter in the market square/school playground/parish grounds/park and be obstructive to villagers and passers-by.
2. Use foul language in everyday conversation and towards villagers – particularly JUNE, MRS WIX, MR JENKINS, LEN, COLIN AND ARTHUR. Foul and abusive language is extremely upsetting and is not required in any circumstances – if I do believe someone has been unjust or stolen my Amazon package, I will see Reverend Seaton first and hopefully we can resolve it in a way that does NOT involve conflict (or eggs, apples or plums).
3. Climb on top of the community centre and jump off the roof for fun. I also promise NOT to encourage other children to do the same. Jumping off the community centre is antisocial and extremely dangerous. Roof tiles have also been damaged and the community centre cannot afford to have these constantly replaced.
4. Block the footpath over the bridge and/or charge 'Bridge tax' from pedestrians wishing to cross.
5. Shoplift from the community stores or any other shop.
6. Throw apples from the parish gardens into the community centre skylight. Karen the cleaner has enough to do without cleaning fermented apple fragments from walls, carpets and windows.
7. Spread rumours about Kenneth the Tesco trolley boy. Kenneth is not a child killer/sex maniac/deformed test-tube-baby science experiment. Spreading rumours about him is vile and deeply upsetting.
8. Play the game 'Suicide by Len' by throwing pine cones at Len while he is sat peacefully on the park bench.

9. Steal people's dogs from outside shops. The owner has tied them up so they can go inside the community stores to do their shopping. This is NOT animal cruelty or neglect, and calling the RSPCA is not only wasting our time but is also wasting theirs.
10. Pour Fanta into the postbox. This is vandalism.
11. Use the public toilets for science experiments.
12. Use Michael Slugs for science experiments.
13. Convince Arthur that June 'fancies him/wants a romantic relationship with him'. This was deeply upsetting for both parties and the confusion ended up in the arrest of Arthur.
14. Cycle backwards down the busy road, for fun.
15. Cycle backwards down the flight of stairs in the village hall, for fun.
16. Draw large hats and bow ties on images of Our Lord Jesus Christ in the church.
17. Answer phone calls from the Reverend's wife Polly, when he's out of the room and pretend to be his mistress/lady of the night.
18. Harass the users of the village mobile-library van. Colin was incredibly upset to be followed back from the van to his front door with us following behind shouting 'Bookworm!'. He later revealed he was unable to read his book in fear of becoming a 'bookworm'.

Signed

KERRY MUCKLOWE
Kerry Mucklowe

Kurtan Mucklowe
Kurtan Mucklowe

Francis Seaton
Witnessed by

Reverend Francis Charles Seaton

I, Reverend Francis Charles Seaton, hereby promise Kerry and Kurtan Mucklowe that I WILL NOT:

1. Call you 'kiddly-winks', especially in public areas. I understand you are both adults and no longer children.
2. Wear Speedos when I take you swimming on Saturdays, and I will invest in a new pair of swimming trunks.
3. Approach you if you are out in the village mingling with friends. I shall keep walking and pretend not to know you.
4. Sing along to songs in the car or tap my thumbs on the steering wheel to the beat of the music.
5. Reminisce or tell you stories about my time at college and my adolescence, and draw comparisons with various crossroads you may have in your own lives.
6. Say the word 'Crimbo' at Christmas time.
7. Tell you to wrap up warm during the colder months. You are adults and can choose what clothes you wear.
8. Slurp my tea loudly.
9. Use the word 'biccies' when talking about biscuits.
10. Let the hairs grow from the top of my nose; I shall pluck them on a regular basis.
11. Tag Kerry or Kurtan in videos on Facebook of animals doing silly things.
12. Wear my bumbag when at Slimbridge Wetland Centre with Kerry and Kurtan.
13. Say 'whoops-a-daisy' when I accidentally spill something.
14. Use 'emojicons' when texting, as I often choose the wrong emojicon for the emotions I'm wanting to display.
15. Sign off text messages with 'LOL', and understand that this means 'laugh out loud' and not 'lots of love'.
16. Park directly outside the youth club when I pick you up; I will instead park around the corner.
17. Clap in the cinema when the film finishes.

Signed

Francis Seaton

Reverend Francis Charles Seaton

KERRY MUCKLOWE

Kurtan Mucklowe

Witnessed by Kerry and Kurtan Mucklowe

Swindon College Prospectus

Choose from a variety of part-time and full-time courses, earning qualifications from A-Levels to GNVQs right through to BA (Hons). All designed to help you get the job you want!

Take advantage of our brand new canteen, boasting lots of new and delicious meals, including homemade lasagne and pesto chicken!

There's still time to apply!

VILLAGE NEWS

Autumn Edition

VILLAGE NEWS

St Mary's Parish

Obituary Former Holly Park School woodwork teacher Mr Dennis Perkins sadly passed away in June after a short illness, at the age of 69. Dennis will be fondly remembered for his positive outlook on life, cheeky sense of humour, warmth and friendliness. He was an active member of the community with his Parish Council work and commitment to the cricket club. Dennis moved to the village in 1973 with wife Betty, raising two children here, Sally and Paul. He leaves behind Betty, who is currently raising money for a bench to be honoured in his name in his favourite part of the village, by Hillbrook Stream, where he spent countless Saturdays staring into space. If interested in contributing, please contact Betty on 769444.

Diamond anniversary

Congratulations to Arthur and Elizabeth Andrews of Colebridge Drive, who will be celebrating their 60th wedding anniversary later this month. Arthur (aged 83) and Margaret (aged 80) have lived in the village for 47 years. They have two children, Robert and Catherine, and Robert's son, Denzil, is expecting Arthur and Elizabeth's first great-grandchild. Perhaps this is something for Arthur to finally smile about!

Crime wave! Most of our villagers will be aware that there has been a spate of petty crime in the village recently, including vandalism at the village hall. A mug belonging to the Scouts was mindlessly chipped and somebody tried to flush an entire roll of Andrex toilet paper down one of the toilets in the gents. The reason why the toilets are called 'the gents' is because they are used in a gentlemanly manner, not a barbaric one. If you know someone who may have been involved in these incidents, please contact PC Webber immediately.

Bus service The Parish Council has been leading a project to reinstate bus services following the withdrawal of the No. 54 in May. Keep your eyes peeled in future newsletters for developments.

Kerry and Kurtan's litter pick

A huge well done to Kerry and Kurtan for their sponsored 24-hour litter pick in the market place on Saturday, which raised £3.57 for St Mary's Church. I think most will agree that we've never seen the market place look so tidy!

Dog mess We've had a few complaints about another increase in dog mess in the village. If you are one of the repeat offenders, please clean up after your dog – and take it home with you, don't leave bags of poo hanging on trees for other people to clean up. For heaven's sake!

Food bank notice This autumn, the church will be hosting a drive for the food bank during the first two weeks of October. We are very grateful for all your donations so far, not to mention the 32 boxes of Cornflakes from local resident David Chadwick. I certainly know a few regular food bank users who will be happy about that!

Tea Talk A brand new initiative is looking for volunteers to give up a couple of hours a week to visit some of our older residents in the village for a nice cup of tea and a chinwag. You might even get a slice of lemon drizzle, if you're lucky!

Len Clifton A few of our residents have voiced their concerns about the night-time activity of resident Len Clifton. I'm quite happy him using the market place as somewhere to sit and spend some hours, but I will be drawing the line at people's personal properties, including gardens, garage spaces and bins. If you do see him, be careful on approach and ring me immediately.

Helping our hedgehogs

June is doing a fantastic job rescuing and caring for our spiky friends, who, year upon year, we see often flattened to death on the road – an all too common sight. With the help of several volunteers, this year she has managed to rescue four hedgehogs from the roadside. And just a reminder: with bonfire night approaching, please build your bonfire on the day it is to be lit and never on top of piles of leaves, as there may be hedgehogs nesting underneath that will burn to an unnecessary crisp. Also, if you find a hedgehog, please do not feed it bread and milk as this bloats them and they have been known to explode because of it, causing an almighty mess.

Autumn Edition

VILLAGE NEWS

St Mary's Parish

A message from Arthur

'As most of you may already know, over the last few years, I have been suffering from chronic stomach pain, which has become so painful I have taken the decision to cut my life short with the help of a euthanasia clinic in Switzerland. Although a tough decision to make, I believe it's in the best interests of my family and I. However, for one night only, you are all invited to my farewell party, where we can celebrate my life and dance the night away! Bon Voyage Mon Amis! Arthur Andrews.' Details of the party will be posted under the 'What's On' section.

Notice

Please ignore continued requests of sponsorship from Kerry and Kurtan for their litter pick, as this has already finished. If any incidents do occur, please contact me.

Baked beans bath for charity

Last Tuesday saw June Winwood and Mrs Wix partaking in an utterly bonkers fundraiser for St Mary's Church by sitting in a bath of baked beans for 2 hours! Mrs Wix said, 'I can't believe I sat in a bath of baked beans for two hours! I'm still finding baked beans in my crevices!' A huge well done to both for their efforts and for raising a whopping £11.85 for charity. Please keep your eyes peeled for future fundraising events, where anyone willing can get involved.

Bowls Club comedy night!

Terry Clarke will be hosting a brand new comedy night at the Bowls Club every last Friday of the month, starting this Friday (27th), with guest headline comedian all the way from Hereford, Harry Ballsack. £3 entry. Warning: Adult humour. Over 18s only.

Bell ringers

Join our dedicated team of bell ringers and become a bell ringer yourself! Here at St Mary's Church we have six large bells that require ringing for various occasions. Why not try it out? Bell ringing for beginners, every Thursday 6pm, St Mary's Church.

What's On

- **Saturday 8th July** @ The Keepers: Live music from rhythm and blues band Mixed Reviews. 8:30–11pm. FREE.

- **Friday 18th Aug** @ The Village Hall: Murder Mystery Night. 7:30–10pm. Tickets £5, from June or Audrey. Dress code: Murder on the Orient Express. Drinks and nibbles provided. Message from June: Please note this event is for fun and not serious, as our last murder mystery night ended up with someone spiking the punch with slug poison. I do not want to be making late-night trips to A&E again dressed as Miss Marple!

- **Saturday 19th Aug** @ The Keepers: John's pub quiz. 7:30pm for 8pm start. Landlord John is running a quiz night for teams of up to 5 people. £5 per team. Cash prizes. John has made it clear that if there are any team names referring to the promiscuity of his wife they will be immediately eliminated.

- **Saturday 26th Aug** @ The Village Hall: Farewell Arthur. 8pm till late. Disco from 9pm. Nibbles provided and Arthur has kindly put £50 behind the bar, so get there early! Message to Len from Arthur: Please don't try and enter wearing a disguise, because you are not welcome.

Wordsearch

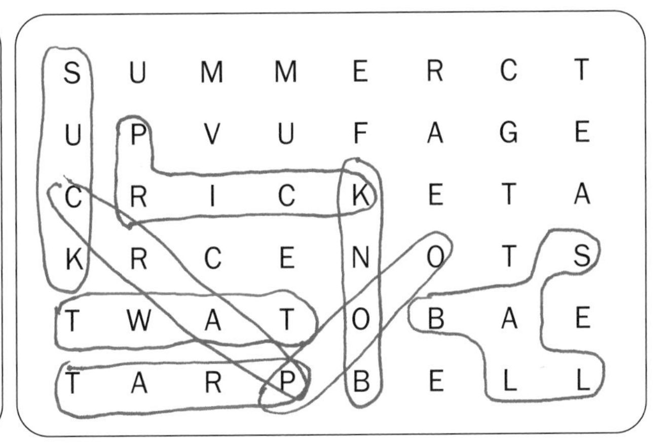

Want to be your own boss?
Earn extra income? Work from home?
Then join Eternal Vitality today and start your journey to success! What are you waiting for?

Eternal Vitality is more than just a business opportunity, it's a way of life. Become a rep and build your own business with Eternal Vitality and earn £££.

Benefit from our proven success and lay the foundations of your own business through our multi-level management scheme. Choose where you work and when you want to work. No more dreaded 6am alarm calls and horrible bosses. Sign up today! You'd be an idiot not to.

Shaz Gallacher – *'Before I became an Eternal Vitality rep, life couldn't get any worse. My house was being haunted by a poltergeist and I was working in a dead-end job for little money and no future, but since becoming an Eternal Vitality rep in 2014, my life has changed for the better.* I'm my own boss, I work from home and earn up to £15,000 a month. Oh, and next month, I'm taking the kids to Disney Land Paris with money I've earned from Eternal Vitality!'*

Be your own boss and join Eternal Vitality now!

Contact us now on 1375 75533, email: eternalvitality@media.org

Terms and conditions:
£200 start-up fee to receive starter pack.12.5% commission on orders over £100 and 15% for orders over £175.
*Eternal Vitality is not responsible for the exorcism of poltergeists.

Sports Update

A successful month was had by our village sports teams, starting with the cricket, where the 1sts ran out victorious over league rivals Fairford. A hefty total of 238 was set before bowling out Fairford for just 87, with Dan Greaves being Man of the Match by taking 4 wickets and scoring 107 runs! Well done, Dan. Despite the win, the day was marred by an incident after the match involving defecation in one of the opposing team member's bicycle helmets. I understand it's healthy to have a bit of sporting rivalry, but this took it too far.

The Keepers won again to keep up their challenge for top spot in the Cotswolds District Men's Skittles League. They ran out 10–2 winners against The Siddington Skittlers and will now face South Cerney this Thursday in the battle for the top two. Team Captain Roger said, *'It was pretty easy really, it was like playing against a bunch of Teletubbies.'*

And a congratulations (of sorts) is in order for Bowls Club member Colin Cresswell, who has won 'Wally of the Week' for the 34th week running! It's a new club record that will take some beating. Bowls Club owner Terry said of the record-breaker: *'He's a wally, that's the long and short of it. He'll stop winning Wally of the Week when he starts screwing his head back on. He's always leaving his bowls gear in away changing rooms.'* Retaining his title will mean poor Colin will have to cough up another £5 fine for charity. *'I can't afford it,'* said Colin, *'I haven't got much money as it is and it's a really big hole in my weekly food budget – to be honest, it's crippling me.'* What a great sport. Long may it continue!

Spot The Ball

Mark an 'x' where you think the ball should be

NEIGHBOURHOOD WATCH

with Kerry Mucklowe

CONFIDENTIAL

I have started a neighbourhood watch in my street as no one else seems to be doing it which I think is really fucking dangerous to be honest. Last week our recycling bin was stolen from outside the front of our house and the week before that an empty tube of sour cream Pringles was forcibly stuffed into the hedge in the front of our garden. I've heard that travellers do this as a sign to other travellers to let them know this property has a dog of value worth stealing. We don't have a dog thank Christ but when my Mum snores it sometimes sounds like a Staffy barking.

8am

Cat seen on the path outside Carol's house. Tabby in look and nature. Tail up, arsehole so clean you could almost see your reflection in it. Sniffed at a cream knitted glove that had been discarded on the side of the road. I put the glove up high on the wall for the rightful owner to collect but has fallen back on floor due to wind/clipped by flying magpie.

9am

Have returned glove to wall, hard for the owner to recognise now as it is now dirty from road. Cat tried sniffing at it again but was frightened away by a leaf blower being started in adjacent road. Glove still not collected, cat arsehole still clean, lifting his tail high as if to show off to everyone/ ward other cats away? Not sure.

9:15am

Elderly man walks past my house. Walking so slowly takes him 20 minutes. Suspicious?

10am

Postman delivered a leaflet for Domino's Pizza and one council tax bill. Odd as he looks exactly the same as he usually does but nose 3x larger than usual? I watched a film last week about shape shifters and it's not unusual for robots to disguise themselves as humans but make a slight mistake with proportions, e.g. nose? Not unusual also that I deleted my Facebook account last week because I was worried about Mark Zuckerberg looking at my private messages. Robot postman with 3x bigger nose sent by Zuckerberg? Domino's leaflet sent as a ploy because he knows I loves Domino's?

11am

Glove still not collected, Red Fiat Panda drives past, followed by yellow Skoda, followed by green Audi. Colours of the rainbow in their exact order? Coincidence? I think not. Probably something to do with that fucking psychopath Zuckerberg – trying to work out connection. Cat sat on path and almost nodded to each car as they drive by. Also a magpie in my front garden, been there for like half an hour yet not interested by a bit of tin foil poking out of our recycling bin? Very unlike magpie no?

12pm

Glove fell down again. Run over by reckless old lady in mobility scooter. Shouted at her from window but she kept on driving like a maniac into town. I'm pretty sure it's Gary Hill's nan, and he goes fucking mental on blue Skittles. This one time we were at parents evening at school and his parents showed up and they were the size of juggernauts. I believe he overdoses on blue Skittles to escape the crippling embarrassment over the size of his gigantic parents.

12:36pm

Kurtan popped in. What at first seemed like a friendly passing visit turned into him just wanting to borrow my PS3 controller. He barely even made the polite chit chat that heroin addicts do to their drug dealers before asking for a 10-bag. I explained to him about the postman with 3x larger nose and he was v interested. We looked up postman on Facebook, his name is Fred Bartlett. We looked at his holiday pictures of Spain in 2013. He looked like he had a great time there. He visited the beach with his wife and they did lots of beach-based activities. They went to some sort of ruins which looked nice and rode on quad bikes. One night they went to a restaurant and had paella and got a picture with the waiter who gave them free shots of limoncello all night. In response to comment left by his mum on picture of waiter, Fred describes 'Carlos' as a 'laugh' and 'lovely host', so much so they ate there every night even though they were booked at an all-inclusive hotel. Why would you flitter money away when you know that there's a decent FREE buffet waiting for you at hotel? All cos of a waiter called Carlos? I think not. Surely the guy can't be THAT much of a laugh. Many a joke must get lost in translation. Picture of Fred stood on balcony in apartment, his eyes are glowing RED like Terminator – not very humanly no? Not seen one picture of him in pool either. I am guessing that's because robots cannot function in water, as water gets into their cogs etc and fucks up their master drive. I guess it's the equivalent to throwing a new laptop in the pool, you just wouldn't do it, would you? I recognise his wife as working in WHSmiths in Cheltenham. It was nice to put the two of them together at last. I wonder whether she has noticed the size of his nose recently or if she's too busy sat on a till with a queue of people waiting whilst complaining to her colleague Tracey saying, 'I should have been on my lunch break 10 minutes ago.'

1pm

Kurtan got bored and started hitting me on head with inflatable microphone that I got as a joke birthday present few years back from my Auntie Linda. I told Kurtan if he's not gonna help in the investigation then it's best if he just leaves. He said he does want to get involved in the investigation but he's not entirely sure what we're investigating. Neither am I to be fair but isn't that the whole point of an investigation?

1:05pm

Kurtan has left with my PS3 controller which I guess I won't be getting back any time soon. But when he does return it I'm sure the buttons will be stuck cos he's spilt Fanta on it. He's so OCD with his own PS3 controllers but utterly reckless with everyone else's.

1:13pm

Don't know how but looking at postman's Facebook page has taken me to the page of a man called Terry Wilson. Terry Wilson's kids are the ugliest things I have ever seen. There is a picture of the youngest on his first day at school and his face looks like an overgrown squash. Facial features so bland and spaced WAY too far apart. I believe that if I took a 15cm ruler and placed it between his eyes there would still be room to fit two pieces of Airways chewing gum lengthways. Imagine being an optician and having to fit a pair of glasses on this freak, you'd just hang yourself.

2pm

Glove still not collected. Cat sniffing the air. Cat ears back as if to say 'What's that smell?' Cat now sleeping under parked van. I hate the way the cat thinks he owns the road. But I suppose he does in the animal kingdom.

3:22pm

GLOVE GONE. Went to the toilet for a really quick dump (2-3 mins MAX), came back and GLOVE GONE. Will investigate and come back when I have more news.

3:23pm

Glove reappeared. Totally my mistake, was looking at the wrong bit of wall when I came back from the toilet.

4pm

Started thinking about Terry Wilson's spaceship-head son. How does one learn to love a child with a head so astronomically large? Have gone back on Facebook to look at more Terry Wilson pictures. Seems he works at Homebase. He's put a picture up on his Facebook of a sale they have at Homebase on garden furniture, as if he's advertising it? Correct me if I'm wrong but surely that's not his job – it's Homebase themselves. Although saying that, I've seen less and less of their adverts on TV. I really hope all is well in the Homebase camp. It's a great chain that has everything under one roof. I hope people don't take this for granted like they did with Toys R Us. The problem with Toys R Us is everyone just went there to browse or have a go on the bikes. The CEOs were like, 'It's all well and good everyone popping in to have a go on our bikes and ride around our store willy-nilly, but no one's buying a fucking single thing.' I think the problem was their prices. They were trying to flog Playmobil pirate ships for like £149 and Sylvanian Family doll houses for £200. I've seen REAL houses in Blackpool go for less than that. I went into the one in Swindon when it had a closing down sale, and it was like a wasteland. They were so desperate I even saw them selling 'Baby on board' car stickers for like 20p. How the mighty have fallen. What the fuck is that giraffe gonna do for work now?

4:47pm

Empty McFlurry pot rolling around in circles in middle of road, which brings up some huge questions as nearest McDonald's is about 15 miles away?? It looks like a Smarties McFlurry. Just did some research and Smarties McFlurrys were discontinued 4 years ago?? This fella has been on one hell of a journey. I bet he's seen some mad stuff. It's like *Homeward Bound* but with a McFlurry cup. I say homeward bound but where is home for this guy? The recycling plant? He deserves more than that, surely, after the shit he's been through. He's living a life of absolute limbo. I'll try and give him a proper burial this afternoon if I remember/can be fucked.

4:54pm

Just had a thought – why can't KFC get their chips right? They've perfected their chicken recipe but the chips are an absolute disgrace. Has no one in the boardroom at KFC ever just sat everyone down and said, 'Guys, the chips just aren't good enough.' The amount of chips I've left behind in a bag of KFC is mind blowing and this is coming from somebody who would still eat a takeout Chinese two days after ordering it.

6pm

Glove still there. Mum shouted down from upstairs. Apparently my Auntie Linda had a dream about our dead nan saying she was unhappy about how her will was dealt with which was odd as she left absolutely fuck all.

7pm

Cooked dinner for me and Mum. We had chicken kievs, chips and beans. I like to put a bit of Reggae Sauce in the beans to spice them up a bit but Mum says it sets her ass on fire. Whatever happened to Levi Roots? I know he sold sauces to all supermarkets in England and they put Reggae Sauce in burgers in Wetherspoons now, but surely he's gotta start comin up with some new ideas soon cos this sauce idea is spreading a bit thin and everyone is only ever gonna know him as the 'sauce guy' which is a sad legacy to leave to his kids. He needs to start thinkin long and hard about what he wants to be known for.

7:26pm

Watching 'The One Show' in the living room with Mum. I wonder if Matt Baker likes the smell of his own farts? Everyone does.

8:03pm

One Show has finished. Back looking out window. Nothing much about. Can see old man in window across the road at No. 56. He looks like the exact double of the old man in *Jurassic Park.* Just started singing the *Jurassic Park* theme tune while watching him put his wet socks on the radiator. Feelin v emotional.

8:32pm

Posted on village 'lost and found' Facebook page about glove. No one has come forward yet. People more interested in post about missing dog last seen in Shepherds Way yesterday morning. Judging from the picture of how sad the whippet looks I reckon it just went off somewhere quietly to die. Must be difficult to determine whether your dog is just plain lost or gone off somewhere to commit suicide. No one ever really talks about dog suicide. It's v taboo.

9:15pm

Dog found! It got stuck between a shed and a wall chasing a leaf. Still no comments on post about glove.

9:43pm

Just seen Len walking down road. Bit late for Len to be out no? Sent by Zuckerberg? Or just stealing people's recycling bins again? He just stopped for a minute to karate-kick a pigeon. Got nowhere near. Cat watched whole thing and had look on its face as if to say, 'You've lost your marbles, mate.'

9:55pm

Len still in road. Looks v shifty. Looking over at our bin. Think he's interested in it. Must be something to do with bit of tin foil poking out of it. Know for a fact Len likes shiny things.

9:56pm

Len's clocked me watching from window and is now pretending not to be interested in our bin. Super-soaker at the ready in case he encroaches on property.

9:58pm

Len trying to distract me by pointing up to sky and shouting, 'Wow look UFO!' Poor distraction technique if I'm honest. Should have used something more believable like, 'Look at that Falcon entangled in the telephone line', cos I would have dropped everything to look at that.

10:45pm

Standoff with Len continues. Neither one has moved for almost an hour. He's waiting for me to go to bed so he can steal bin but what he doesn't know is I've just necked 3 Beroccas and washed them down with a whole can of Relentless. I AIN'T SLEEPIN TONITE MATE.

11:14pm

Len clutches chest like he's having heart attack and falls on floor. Suspect it's a ploy to distract me so he can steal bin. Poor from him.

11:34pm

Len still on floor. Hasn't moved now for 20 minutes. Cat biting his trousers. Bit worried. Think I will go down to see if he's alright.

11:38pm

Went outside to help Len but LEN HAS GONE AND BIN GONE! Can't believe I fell for that. He's had my pants down there, to be fair.

The Cotswold
Amateur Theatrical Society (CATS)

present

An Inspector Calls

Directed by Reverend Francis Seaton.
Mon 14th to Sat 19th August 7:30pm,
Sat Matinee 2:30pm.

Tickets available from the village shop,
£7 each.

Starring Reverend Francis Seaton as
'Inspector Goole' and June Winwood as
'Sybil Birling'.

'Fun for all the family! Three stars!'
– The Wilts and Glos Standard.

'Entertaining performance by our cherished Reverend, Francis Seaton'
– Parish Council Newsletter.

Computer – Including all the
bits and that. £50. Will NOT
accept offers.
CALL Mandy Harris 1223 890777.
NO TIME WASTERS/PISS-TAKERS.

SEEKING:

One Baby Oleg from smoke-free and pet-free home. Must be in new condition. Will pay cash or exchange for other Compare the Meerkat characters.

CALL Mandy Harris on 1223890777

NO TIME WASTERS / PISS TAKERS

PET PORTRAITS by Mandy Harris

Will draw any brand of **DOG/CAT**. Can do **HAMSTERS** but would rather not, as cannot get scale right on hands.

PERFECT GIFT – for loved ones.

Price depends on size of pet.

CALL Mandy Harris on 1223890777

NO TIME WASTERS / PISS TAKERS

POEMS BY THE PARISH POND

by Reverend Francis Seaton

Poems by the Parish Pond

One of my favourite pastimes is to indulge in a spot of poetry, when time permits. Nothing gets me more aroused than wetting the quill and putting pen to paper on a new poem of whatever inspires me in that moment. Had I not been a vicar, I would like to think I could have caused quite a stir in the poetry world. Here is a selection of some of my favourite work. (Disclaimer: Best enjoyed accompanied by a steaming hot cup of Earl Grey and a slice of lemon drizzle, in front of a roaring fire.)

'The Waltz of the Tadpole'

by Reverend Francis Seaton

Spring, with all its scents
  and brimming fauna, spills out.
Tadpoles pop like tiny lit embers from
  their once sleepy pods, and dart about
  the parish pond.
Bright eyed, twisting and turning like
  sparrows on a freshly ploughed field
  – so grateful to be alive.
A handful of tadpoles so tiny, so minuscule,
  yet so full of God's will, dance about in
  merriment – they begin the tadpole waltz!
'Oh God Almighty!' they cry,
  'Thank you for this gift of life.'
For no creature, no plant, no bacterium was
  pure accident – 'twas all God's design.
Even a tapeworm, deemed a parasite
  to all, is just another living creature
  trying to get by, In God's heavenly eye.

Afternote: 'The Waltz of the Tadpole' was written by me one spring morning as I sat on the bench beside the parish pond, writing my latest sermon, when I noticed how lively the freshly hatched tadpoles were. They danced about the pond as if they were waltzing, and it dawned on me how important all God's creatures are, no matter how small, how insignificant.

It was that evening I made the decision to no longer use Dettol to clean the work surfaces in my house. Dettol kills 99.9 per cent of bacteria – who am I to decide that these living bacteria should die? Then later that evening, as I was watching television with my wife, Polly, God sent me a sign. I saw an advert for a yoghurt called 'Yakult' that contained good bacteria, which help with your digestive system. I smiled to myself. God has an answer for everything. Now I only use natural lemon juice to clean my surfaces. It's inexpensive, smells lovely, and leaves my tiles with a natural sparkle. Thank you again, Lord!

by Reverend Francis Seaton

'Chaos at Harvest' *by Reverend Francis Seaton*

This next poem, which is a bit of fun really, is about the chaos of our Parish Harvest. What seems at the time to be a very stressful period is rather quite funny, in hindsight!

The Harvest table was bursting with colour,
To the children it brought lots of grins.
There were peaches and apples
and butternut squashes,
But we can't have fresh food – we need tins!

How will we ship this all to Romania?
In the lorry, it's likely to perish.
'You should have been more accurate
on the parish poster,'
Said councillor Nigel, with relish.

In a dash, I headed to the allotments,
Before the villagers dug up their crop.
But Arthur had already harvested
his prize marrow
And when I told him, he got into a bit of a strop.

He threw his marrow into the parish
pond in anger,
The villagers were ready for a brawl.
They held a meeting at the local gardening club,
And voted to NOT donate to the harvest at all!

So Polly drove me to the out-of-town Tesco,
And I piled lots of tins in my trolley.
I spent 324 pounds of my own money,
Which caused a huge row with Polly.

But at least the Romanian orphans
Will have a break from the abuse,
And see the goodness that God preaches,
While they dig in to some delicious tin peaches!

This poem does exactly what it says on the tin!
It's also a true story.

‘An Impromptu Funeral’ *by Reverend Francis Seaton*

Early evening ramble.
The sun sets, a misty amber
  over shimmering golden fields.
A red grouse pops its head above the wheat,
He nods, I nod back.
There’s a tinge of sadness there, but for what?
A snipe glides overhead, bringing in
  the evening clouds,
He glides a figure-of-eight above me.
Almost in salute, but for what?
Then I notice.
A red-legged partridge mourning
  a poor pheasant,
His cadaver just a jumble of bloodied feathers,
Thrown into the undergrowth by the busy road.
A black grouse steps out
  from behind an old oak,
He bows his head for his late friend,
Then scratches with his feet
  fresh dirt over the corpse.
‘Would you like me to conduct a service?’ I ask.
  They nod.
‘God gave you wings, pheasant,’ I begin,
‘But some would say you are a flightless bird,
God only gave you wings to fly the short
  distance to heaven.’

Afternote: This poem was actually published in the monthly Three Counties Parish *magazine. I was so chuffed, I had it framed alongside a feather of our dear late pheasant and hung it on the wall in our downstairs loo. I can officially say I’m a published poet!*

'Think of Us Newts' *by Reverend Francis Seaton*

This next poem, I must admit, is some of my darkest work. Sometimes you have to shock to make a change. I was absolutely beside myself to discover a discarded Lilt can floating in the parish pond, with a newt so entangled in the ring pull I had to (and there's no nice way of putting this) stamp on it to put it out of its misery. The Lilt can was only the start of a series of wildlife massacres I encountered that summer. I wrote this poem to ward off the serial litterers responsible.

Think of us newts when you choose to litter,
The Lilt once sweet has now turned bitter,
I'm a little peckish, I'm not yet full,
Here, let me choke upon this ring pull.

Think of us voles when you throw out
your detritus,
It's as lethal to us as meningitis.
This rusty tin can that once held butter beans,
Has now become my death guillotine.

Think of us hedgehogs when you
toss away your crisp packet,
Or worse, your plastic library book jacket!
'Hey, this sleeping bag looks great!'
Said the hedgehog before he suffocates.

Think of us ducks before you throw away
your rubber bands,
We're only ducks, we don't understand
That this rubber-band necklace may look loose,
But as soon as it slides down our necks, it
becomes our noose.

How much more blood must there be spilled?
How many more of God's creatures must be
killed?
Before this poem ends, let this sink in,
It's only a seven-yard walk to the bin.

Afternote: I laminated this poem and pinned it up on a tree next to the parish pond. The day after, I discovered it tossed in the bin. Well, maybe something got through to them at last!

© Francis Seaton

WELCOME
GOOD BYE
© Francis Seaton

'Guests in Nature's House' *by Reverend Francis Seaton*

Often in life we are let down by things that are sometimes inconsistent, whether it be a friend, a family member or a rather monotonous episode of 'Antiques Roadshow'. In this case, I am often let down by my mother-in-law and, specifically, her attitude to persons of colour. Polly's mother, Joan, often stays with us at various times during the year, but unfortunately stays longer than my patience can stand. As my late father once said, 'House guests are a lot like fish; after three days they start to stink.' And he's quite right. This got me thinking about the things that never outstay their welcome, like the four seasons, for example. In fact, seasons are a lot like guests in one's house, nature's house. Never staying too long, or not long enough. And when one guest leaves, another arrives, as prompt as the one before. So this next poem is suitably titled 'Guests in Nature's House':

Summer comes and summer goes,
Autumn's here, bright leaves glow,
Then winter comes and winter goes,
And onto spring where new life grows.
Then summer comes back round again,
And autumn, winter and spring again,
They come and go just like a mouse,
Welcomed guests in nature's house.
But neither one stays too long,
Cos if they did, that would be wrong,
Off goes summer, suitcase in hand,
Till next year, he's got other plans.
Oh, here comes autumn, he likes to stay
For just three months, then he's away,
Just like winter and spring, too,
Never outstay their welcome,
  like some guests do.

'An Ode to My Son' *by Reverend Francis Seaton*

This next poem always makes me rather emotional. I wrote it as a birthday present for my son Jacob and read it out in front of him and all his friends at his 18th birthday party. It's about being a father and all the emotion that brings. And there is also a hidden, more practical message in this poem that is important for all young men.

I know it's not 'cool' to say 'I love you'
But son, I'll shout it from the rooftops
if I have to
For you, my boy, are a part of me
That part of me that grew from seed
And as you grow more every day
I love you more in every way
For you, my child, you have my eyes
My sudden temper, sometimes unwise
And everything else that you'll inherit
My balding head, my faults and merits
You are me, you are my son
This father's love can't be undone
And I'm sorry, son, if sometimes I nag
But that's just part of being a dad
And as a dad I have to say
Don't forget to check your prostate
You'll need your glands like I needed mine
For a son of your own like I had mine
A daughter, too, and a loving wife
You'll no longer need your Dad in your life
And when the day comes and I pass on
Don't weep for me although I'm gone
I'm still there, I'm a part of you
I'm in your seed that you pass on too.

© Francis Seaton

LETTERS FROM A SPONSORED DOG

with Big Mandy

Head Office
55 Rivermead Road,
London, EC2D 0GY
www.dogtrust.co.uk

Hi **Mandy Harris**,

My name is Digby the Lurcher. Thank you so much for sponsoring me.

When I first came to the Dog Trust, I was severely underweight and had quite bad eyesight due to an infection. The first seven years of my life have been rather tough for me, but I still have lots of love to give.

Your **£5** a month will help pay towards:

- Veterinary bills

- Food for my healthy, balanced doggy diet

- Blankets and toys for my very own kennel

I am receiving lots of love from the staff at the Dog Trust. I go on three walks a day with my other doggy companions and I also get regular check-ups to make sure my health is in tip-top condition!

Thank you so much again, I now get the second chance at life I deserve.

Lots of wet noses and kisses,

Digby x

Dear Digby,

Ur welcome. I've had a tough life and all so kno how you feel. When I was 8 I fucked around with a Ouija board and ever since then I've been tormented by a spirit called Jack Dawkins who was a drummer boy in the first world war who got sniped between the eyes. I've suffered from insomnia cos he literally levitates above my bed every night staring at me whilst playing a never ending drum roll. I've asked him to stop but all he ever says is 'Hurt you, hurt you'. And no one believes me. Do u kno how fuckin isolating that is?

So how you findin it in the kennels and that? Is it like bein inside? Ur more than welcome to come and crash here for a couple of days. But I suspect it would be a long drive for you comin from Lancashire and that. Just to let you know i would stay well away from wet food cos it rots your teeth like my Tysons. And how's your eyesight holdin up? That infection fucked your eyes? Or can you see shadows and that? Fair play to u mate.

All the best,

Mandy Harris

Head Office
55 Rivermead Road,
London, EC2D 0GY

www.dogtrust.co.uk

Hi **Mandy**, it's Digby, your sponsor dog here!

Just a quick update on my progress.

I'm doing great, as you can see in my picture enclosed. I'm loving my daily walks and I'm slowly becoming more confident around people and other dogs. I'm now at a healthy weight and my sight is gradually improving.

Your monthly sponsorship has given me a new lease of life. Thank you for helping me on my journey to happiness.

Lots of wet noses and kisses,

Digby x

Hi Digby,

Don't ask me any questions then. I basically spilled my guts out to you in that last letter and all you can do is go on about yerself. Friendship is a two way street not a one way street where you talk about yourself and your fucking eyesight the whole time. Im not doin too great thanks for askin. Anxiety through the roof. Paranoid as hell. And now I'm havin flashbacks to the time I nearly died at thorpe park. Oh you dont know how I nearly died at thorpe park? Well why would you? YOU NEVER ASKED. Would be nice to hear sum kind words from u regardin my situation. As i said more than welcome to crash at mine any time and watch films. have u ever seen homeward bound? wot are ur thoughts on it? is the acting any good from the dogs? difficult to judge as a human. shame cos I don't think I've seen any of them in anythin else since. they must be in their 40's now. actually I tell a lie, the Labrador made a brief appearance in the film 'sherlock bones' but not as a lead character.

All the best,

Mandy Harris

p.s. tyson has got a joke for u. How do u know if ur a slow dog? u chase parked cars LOL.

Head Office
55 Rivermead Road,
London, EC2D 0GY

www.dogtrust.co.uk

Hi **Mandy**, it's Digby, your sponsor dog here!

You're going to be super-surprised when I tell you my great news — I've found a new home! I'm ever so excited because I'll be going to live with a lovely family who have plenty of experience with Lurchers.

I've been at the Dog Trust now for three years so I'm going to miss lots of people — especially my wonderful carers. I'm going to miss you, too, and I hope you won't be too upset. My new start in life wouldn't have been possible without all your love and support, so thank you for making me so waggy!

I do hope you'll continue your sponsorship with one of my doggy pals. My friend Seamus has been here at the Dog Trust for two years and is seeking sponsorship. He's a five-year-old Jack Russell. You can read all about him in the enclosed certificate.

Thanks again for being such a wagtastic friend to me; it's only thanks to your support that the Dog Trust has been able to give dogs like me the second chance we deserve.

Wags and licks,

Digby x

Certificate of Sponsorship

This is to certify that

Mandy Harris

... a dog at the Dog Trust

Dear Seamus,

Fort I'd give you a heads up on your so called mate Digby. DO NOT TRUST HIM. At first he'll act like he's really interested in you but all he's interested in is HIMSELF and MONEY. M-O-N-E-Y. Specifically YOUR money. He'll take it and run for the hills. He don't give a fuck who's heart he breaks along the way. He's a massive narcissist basically and there's no room in his heart to love anyone other than himself. We have been pals for 3 months and he's sucked the entire life out of me. I kno this is probably hard to hear but I wish someone had dun the same for me when I first got involved with him.

I'm pretty much resigned to the fact I'll never get my money back, but it's the massive head fuck i'm left still dealing with. Anyway, you'll probably ignore this coz you think 'Digby's alright? I've never had any problems with him?' but thats exactly how he first suckers you in.

Revenge is not in my plans cos he'll fuck himself on his own.

All the best,

Mandy Harris

MEMOIRS OF A KURTAN

by Kurtan

MY
HEART

Wednesday 1st Jan

My New Years resolution is to start keeping a diary. I figured that in centuries to come when people read it they might finally understand what a tortured genius I was.

Sunday 5th Jan

Watched the film "6th Sense" today with Nan but I missed the line 'I see dead people' when I went for a slash. Realised that film means nothin without that line. I was just sat there watchin & thinkin 'what's the plot twist in this film cos he's just seein people that are alive??'

Tuesday 14th Jan

Last night I had a dream there was a terrorist attack in the village and the church got blown up. Then these people went in the village shop and tied up Mrs Wix and shoved an entire carton of sour Nerds into her mouth until she ended up sucking her entire mouth up into her brain. And during the fete a bloke dressed all in black defecated in the tombola and people were just pulling out bits of turd, then the terrorists got the vicar and put his body on the hog roast and everyone was just carvin bits off it. Last time I had a premonition like this was when Woolworths closed down. I remember sayin to Kerry 'Woolworths is gonna close down' and she goes 'no way they've got too many shops all over the country' and I said 'watch this space'. A week later Woolworths closed down and I remember when I heard the news I literally just collapsed in the middle of the street.

Thursday 23rd Jan

Walked in the woods behind Kerry's house today. Hadn't been there in years. I reckon the last time I was there was when it was just me and Darren Lacey one summer holidays dickin about and Darren Lacey got pissed eatin a fermented apple that he found on the ground and passed out under a tree. I was shittin myself cos I couldn't get him home and I knew we would be in so much trouble. That was the beginning of the end for me and Darren Lacey I think, cos he was too much of a liability.

Saturday 25th Jan

Just found out my house is haunted. I left twenty quid on the side in my bedroom last night and after Kerry came over it completely vanished. Couldn't find it anywhere.

Thursday 6th Feb

I was clearing out the drawers in my room today and found my old Goosebumps book 'Say Cheese or Die'. The thing about R.L Stine is he gets into your mind and proper fucks with it. Last time I read one of his books I got a panic attack and I only read up to the contents page.

Friday 14th Feb

Valentines Day. No cards, surprise surprise. Don't care anyway. Vicar took me and Kerry to McDonalds in Cheltenham to cheer me up which got me thinkin... finding love is a lot like tryin to win at McDonalds Monopoly. You gotta put the graft in to get results. You can't be peeling your stickers expectin to win a Mini and a trip to the Balearic islands when you've only paid for a medium extra value meal cos you won't, you'll win a small fries or even worse a soggy fruit bag at best. You gotta do your groundwork, check other tables to see if people left their stickers on their drinks, check the bins, invest in the board, play the long game, cos you'll be surprised that not many people play the long game, cos they can't be assed. Which is why when it pops up on Facebook "People you might know", I poke every single bird on there until it runs out of birds I might know. It's a small thing but by doing it I increase my chances of porkin tenfold.

Sunday 2nd March

I asked my Nan to get me some chocolate from the shop and she came back with a Wispa. I hate Wispas. If I get a selection box at Christmas I always eat the Wispa last. Curly Wurly, Chomp, Freddo then Wispa. I leave it right till the last, I won't even eat the Wispa over the Christmas period, I'll eat it in January, and only when I'm absolutely desperate. I'd rather break my teeth on a thousand Dime bars than put a Wispa near my lips.

Saturday 8th March

Saw Len today sat on the bench outside the church and when I was chatting to him I swear I could hear the sound of a whirring camera coming from inside his head which got me thinking that my life was the Truman Show and the entire village was the studio set and the pigeons had cameras in them and that. So I thought if I walked as far as I could out the village I'd just hit a wall. I got as far as Burford, then just got bored and walked back.

Friday 21st March

Went to the new Harvester today in Malmesbury with Nan and I can tell you now I won't be going again for a simple reason and that reason is SALAD BARS. I hate salad bars... People use the wrong tongs for the wrong salads... and they end up contaminating the potato salad with the bacon bits... they just use the same tongs for everything... lunacy.

Wednesday 9th April

The fat on old men's necks that hang over the collar of their shirts make me wanna barf.

Wednesday 14th May

Saw Farmer Jenkins in the shop earlier this morning and I told him I was competing in the scarecrow festival this weekend and he just goes really arrogantly 'good luck with that'. And I said 'cheers Jenkins, is your wife still dead?' And he goes 'Yeah', and I go 'good luck with that'.

Tuesday 20th May

Watched a documentary last night with Nan about witch finders in the olden times. It made me think that Kerry is really lucky she weren't born back in those days cos she definitely would have been accused of being a witch cos of her great big nose. Personally, I would have stayed well clear of the witch finder general. I would probably have been a humble basket weaver and kept to myself but perhaps occasionally frequented the local tavern.

Saturday 19th July

went to the village Summer fete today and it was pure carnage. Basically one of the barn owls got loose from the owl display, and it swooped and snatched this half eaten hotdog that was just lying on the floor and all the towns folk was screamin at it, then it flew and landed on a mug tree on the white elephant stall and it just sat there eatin this hotdog in a terrifyin manner. And everyone was losin their shit including the vicar so Darren Lacey went home and got his crossbow and shot it dead and now the owl display people reckon he owes them two grand. But that ain't the end of it cos apparently Darren Lacey got out of payin it cos he said he thought the hotdog the owl was eatin was a two-month-old human baby. And then after the fete Darren Lacey Facebooked me sayin he KNEW the hotdog the owl was eatin WAS a hotdog. He only said he thought it was a two-month-old baby cos he wanted to use his new crossbow cos he just got his crossbow licence.

Thursday 14th August

I've only ever cried twice in my life. Once was when Kerry sang 'Bring Him Home' at my Grandad's funeral and today at 2pm when I caught my pubes on some parcel tape.

Friday 15th August

Just had a mad thought. Cos life expectancy is getting higher and higher does that mean one day 60-year-olds will be considered teenagers? And 90-year-olds will be going through a midlife crisis? There will probably be so many old people on this planet that the queues at the post offices will stretch for miles and miles and miles and Werthers Originals will run out and phone scamming businesses will absolutely boom and the Queen will only send cards to people who live to a thousand years old. There will be so few young people that old people will have no one to tell off.

Saturday 16th August

Darren Lacey said that at Burford Wildlife Park there's a carpark there for 280 cars and 12 coaches and the carpark used to be manned by this little Italian fella with a withered arm called Gianni. So Gianni right used to go round the carpark charging cars a quid and coaches five quid to park there and basically Gianni had worked there for 25 years and one day he just didn't turn up for work. So Burford Wildlife Park phoned up the local council to send them a new car parking attendant and the council were like 'that carpark is your responsibility?' and Burford Wildlife Park were like 'Is it?? I thought Gianni was employed by the council??' and the council were like 'Uh...no? Who the fucks Gianni??' So sitting in his massive villa somewhere in Italy smoking a cigar with his withered arm is Gianni who's been taking the parking fees at Burford Wildlife Park estimated at about £400 per day for the past 25 years. I worked out added together that is about 3.6 million pounds and no one even knows if his real name is Gianni cos they didn't wanna come across as racist for questioning it. The man's a fuckin inspiration. Me and Kerry are gonna try and do this at the Village Hall carpark.

Saturday 6th September

Went shoppin today at TK Maxx with Kerry and it made me think... shoppin at TK Maxx is a lot like panning for gold. You don't get unbelievable bargains without sweating your bollocks off in the process. Thought I'd write down a few tips:

Number 1 – Stand your ground. You can't get intimidated by other bargain hunters riflin through the same rail as you towards the Ben Sherman double breasted blazer you got your eye on. Do the 'block and reach'. I'm blockin off his view of the bargains here and I'm reachin for the Ben Sherman double breasted blazer there.

Number 2 – When lookin at the rail, your bargains don't begin and end at eye level. Look underneath, there will be plenty of bargains that have slipped off their hangers and onto the floor. I found a t-shirt on the floor with a boot stamp on it. It was a Calvin Klein. I took it to the counter and showed them the boot prints, they gave me a further £5 reduction.

Number 3 Be open minded. There's no point goin into TK Maxx sayin 'I want to find a black Nike Air Max T-shirt in a size medium to large' cos that ain't gonna happen and it's that sort of pig headedness that will stop you finding the illuminous green No Fear T-shirt that you never knew you wanted.

Number 4 - And lastly, I know it's a small thing but make sure the sales assistant removes the security tags at the counter before leavin the shop cos it will save you the embarrassment at the exit when half a dozen nosy old crows stand there rubber neckin at ya while the security guard goes through your bag.

Sunday 5th October

Apparently Darren Lacey's cousin's mate went to this nightclub in Stroud and he was dancing on the dancefloor and he felt this prick in his leg but thought nothin of it... and anyway later on when he got home and he was gettin into bed he looked down and there was a little cocktail stick stickin out his leg with a little flag on it sayin 'welcome to the world of Aids'. So he was just dancin on the danc floor and someone injected him with Aids.

Monday 6th October

I saw my ex Kirsty Taylor today for the first time since we left school. She was working in the reptile department at Pets at Home in Swindon. It must be nice for her being amongst fellow snakes and cold-blooded reptilians. I saw her feeding a locust to a bearded dragon - It's funny cos a few years ago, I was in exactly the same position as that locust. She sucked the life out of me and left nothing but an empty husk. When I asked her where the hamster sawdust was she looked right through me as if she never even knew me and said 'Sally? Sally? where do we keep the hamster sawdust?' to which the woman who had the physical frame of a bowling ball grunted 'by the tills'. Kirsty Taylor was the love of my life. People say 'how can she be the love of your life when you only went out with her for half a day?'... but when you know, you know. We were just a couple of star-crossed lovers in Year 8, foolishly in love. I asked her out on the coach on our school trip down to Hampton Court Palace and on the way back she dumped me for Jack Russell. She fucked me over massively and to be honest I don't think I've ever recovered from it. Here's a letter I wrote to her a few years after she dumped me. I never sent it in the end but it helped me get a lot of the anger out and because of that her name has dropped down 3 places in my most searched Facebook profiles.

Kirsty... I've been going over and over and over in my head what went wrong. You seemed fine when you were holding my hand as we walked round the maze but as soon as we stepped back on that coach something had changed. You changed. When we first met, you fooled me into thinking you loved me for me, but after being with you for a few hours it was blatantly obvious the only thing you wanted from me was my money. If you had any heart left you would refund me the £1.50 I spent on that bookmark I got you from the giftshop. I hope you enjoyed the money you squeezed out of me cos you won't be getting another dime. Good luck finding someone else's paper-round money to spunk willy nilly on historical bookmarks.

Maybe we just weren't realistic when we were looking at our potential future together. After we talked about our plans for the future (where to sit on the coach on the way home) it became obvious to me and probably to you too that our futures didn't match up. We want different things. I wanted to sit in the front cos I get car sick but you wanted to sit at the back cos you don't give a damn about my illness. I don't think in the whole of our relationship you asked me a single question about myself yet it's funny how I know all the names of your guinea pigs, alive and deceased, Harlow, Mimsy, Freckles, Chandler and Bug Eyes. How is Bug Eyes by the way? Is his body still rejecting his eyeballs?

The truth is Kirsty, even from the beginning I knew deep down I was always going to be second best to your cycling proficiency exam. I understand that certificate meant the world to you but I hoped that one day you'd learn to love me more. The way you treat me is wrong Kirsty, if you don't realise the way you treat me is wrong then I suggest going to therapy to figure out why you treat the people you love the way you do. If you keep putting your cycling proficiency first you're gonna find yourself alone with nowhere or no one to cycle to.

What did Jack Russell have that I didn't other than having the same name as a make of dog and a packet of Maoams? Everyone knows he goes through girls like he does Transformer Snacks, and you'll just be another crisp packet stuffed in the hedge by the science block. Will you seriously be happy with having to sit down and watch him play football every lunch time while he ignores you and occasionally boots the ball in your direction? If you are then I feel sad for you.

Good luck with your cycling proficiency Kirsty. I'll know you'll smash it... your bike I mean... under a bus.

Lots and lots of hate,

Kurtan x

Thursday 9th October

The film 'The Terminal' with Tom Hanks is on TV today which I'm excited about cos I ain't seen it before and I've heard it's a bit of a weeper. I think they've really upped their game Channel 5 in the last couple of years... I'd actually go as far to say it's my second favourite channel after Dave.

Tuesday 21st October

Read somewhere today that in Scotland if someone knocks on your door and asks to use your toilet, the law says you must let them enter otherwise they are legally allowed to piss through your letterbox. Note to self - must try out on Len asap.

Monday 31st October

Apparently Darren Lacey said Slugs and Kayleigh were invited to a masked Halloween party at the Village Hall and before they were about to leave Kayleigh got a migraine and she told Slugs to go to the party alone. So Slugs ended up going to the party alone wearing his pumpkin costume while Kayleigh had a nap. But when she woke up her migraine had gone so she decided to go to the party dressed as Catwoman and since Slugs didn't know what her costume was, she thought she would have some fun by watching how Slugs acted when she werent with him. Then apparently she saw Slugs trying to pork loads of women on the dancefloor so she grabbed him by his throat, got him into the village Hall toilets and shagged him to show Slugs what he was missing. And after that she just fucked off home to bed and he stayed at the party for a bit. Kayleigh was sitting up in bed reading a book when Slugs came in and she goes to him 'did you have a good time at the party?' and he said 'I didn't bother going in the end, I lent my pumpkin costume to Arthur and I just went down the Keepers and played pool.' Then Kayleigh was like 'fuck, I just shagged Arthur in a pumpkin costume'... And apparently Arthur was parading round the Bowls club with a massive smile on his face the next day as if to say 'my nob still works.'

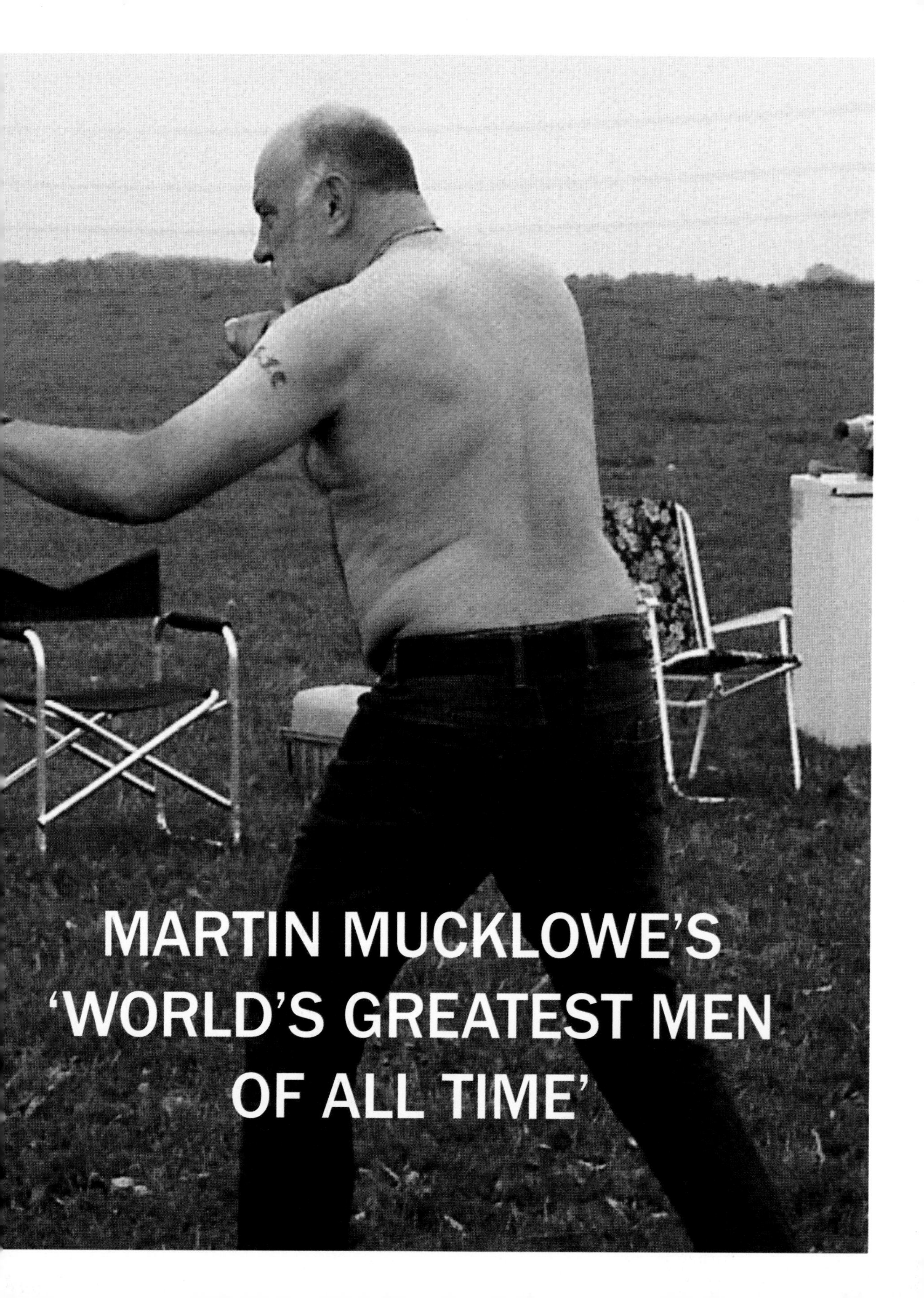

MARTIN MUCKLOWE'S 'WORLD'S GREATEST MEN OF ALL TIME'

Martin Mucklowe's

'World's greatest Men of All Time'

Without men there wouldn't be a single man on this planet, therefore I am celebrating us kind with a list of the greatest of my species. I ain't a woofter, though, let's just say that first!! I like me women and I like me tits but I'm not ashamed to doff my cap to those great men who made Martin Mucklowe what Martin Mucklowe is today.

Tommy from Ground Force

Hard grafter. Good landscape gardener. Like mine, his favourite tipple is a pint of Baileys. Met him once in the toilets at Banbury services. The only man who could come close to me in the trouser department. The man's packing some serious pipe. Last time I saw a wang like that was on a donkey at Weston-super-Mare. Top-notch bloke. Firm handshake. Piss like a carwash jet stream.

Jimmy Nail

Sterling actor. Exceptional singer. The sort of bloke you wouldn't mind sharing a woman with, as long as he kept to his end. I brought my very own pair of crocodile shoes because of the man. I remember walking into the Keepers wearing them for the first time and all the women slid off their bar stools cos they were so wet. Me and Alan ended up having a punch up in the bogs cos Alan's wife kept grabbing at me nob.

Great white shark

Although not a man, I can't do a World's Greatest list without putting a shark in there. Undoubtedly the greatest man of all the animals. Great white sharks have such a strong sense of smell that they can detect a colony of seals two miles away, much like me with a gaggle of women who need their cobwebs dusting off with my massive duster. It's films like *Jaws* that give great white sharks a bad press, but if you actually met a shark like I have you'll find out they're just decent hard working blokes, and eating a human being is equivalent to us eating a bacon sandwich and you don't see bacon sandwiches making horror movies about us! I did a Facebook personality test once and the results came back certifying that I was 90% Megalodon (the largest and extinct species of shark that lived approximately 23 to 26 million years ago). My sense of scent is so strong that I could walk into the Keepers blindfolded and know whether it's John or Julie behind the bar. How, you ask? Cos I can smell women's pheromones through their clothes – even through thermals. I can sniff out if a woman is on her period or not, as long as she's within a hundred yard radius of me and there's not a strong wind.

Percy Shaw

When it's the early hours of the morning and I'm weaving back and forth across the road driving my van after a late night lock-in at the Keepers, I thank the Lord for Percy Shaw, the inventor of cat's eyes. He probably saves my life on average three times a week. Nice one Percy!

Pheebus Mucklowe

My great great great great great great great grandfather Pheebus is a hero of mine. During the great plague of 1665 everyone in the village got wiped out, apart from Pheebus Mucklowe. So Pheebus did the honourable thing and sacrificed himself by fornicating with anything he could get his hands on until his seed repopulated the village. He died shortly after of nob rot but today if you look up any villager's family tree you'll find old Pheebus right at the top of it looking down, proud as punch to have passed down his almighty trunk. I'm proud to be a Mucklowe. We might not be the sharpest lemons on the tree but we're survivors. Throw a stampede of sheep at us and we'll come out riding them like roller-skates.

Kryten from Red Dwarf

Cracks me up. Keeps a cool head despite the crazy Cat's antics.

Roy Chubby Brown

Saw him in the Torquay Palladium one summer in the mid 90s and haven't laughed like that since. He's so quick on his feet and observational, he pointed at my mother-in-law who was sat next to me in the audience and called her a big fat cow – it brought the entire auditorium to a standing ovation. Unfortunately, these days you hear little of him. Like the great man Jim Davidson, another victim of the PC brigade. But as Roy Chubby would say, 'Have you ever seen a good looking feminist?' – and the answer is NO, they're all fat ugly cows.

Odd Job

The Chinese dwarf villain in the Bond film *Goldfinger.* Has a hat with a blade in it. Love the idea of killing someone with a hat.

Geoff Capes

Former Britain's Strongest Man, gold medallist athlete and all-round brick shit house. During his peak he was a tank, no one could touch him. He could lift a chinook above his head with one hand and still be able to sniff his armpit to check for BO. Time has been a cruel mistress, however, and now the poor sod looks like a deflated hot-air balloon fallen on a bird cage. He's got so much saggy skin that when he coughs he looks like a lava lamp.

Rick Parfitt

The guitarist and singer in the band Status Quo. He was the greatest songwriter of my generation and also a personal friend of mine. Here's a little trivia for you: the lyrics 'Down down deeper and down' in the song 'Down Down' was inspired by him watching me drilling his wife at one of his swinging sex parties that he used to hold in his basement every last Saturday of the month. I drilled her so far into the ground she needed an industrial corkscrew to get her out.

Don Rogers

Swindon Town's most legendary player, nicknamed 'The Don', which is also a good description for his business affairs, if you get my drift.

Chris Barrie

The one man responsible for the resurrection of Great British comedy. Never has a sitcom depicted the true chaos of a local leisure centre more than 'The Brittas Empire'. I used to play squash every Wednesday back in 1995 at my local leisure centre but the receptionist never used to know what court was bloody free cos she was too busy watching episodes of 'Gladiators' on a portable television. She had a lovely pair of honks, mind. I actually saw her again working at Argos just a few months ago, but unfortunately her honks had drooped down to plonks. They were so low only the Devil could tickle them with his pitchfork.

John Lowe

The first player to win the World Darts Championship in three separate decades and the first to get a televised nine-dart finish. However, that's not the reason he's in my Top 10 Greatest Men. In the early 90s, Rob used to drink down the Keepers as he was porkin out some bird who worked in the bakery next door and he was the only man ever to go pint to pint with myself.

Myself, Martin Mucklowe

(I know it's not the done thing, but if I don't do it, someone else probably will, so I'm including myself in this list of World's Greatest Men.) Born in 1957, Martin was already famous amongst the female nurses at the hospital for having a member longer than his umbilical cord, so much so that one nurse got confused and almost cut the old boy in half! Martin flourished in everything he turned his hand to, particularly concreting.

Martin is also the only man on this planet who can:

- Blow up a water bottle with his own lungs cos they're so strong.
- Make a woman have an orgasm simply by chalking a pool cue at the Keepers.
- Metabolise a pint in under 5 minutes.
- Run 60mph if he really wanted to.
- Punch a hole in a breeze block.
- Manipulate a fruit machine to pay out a hundred grand.

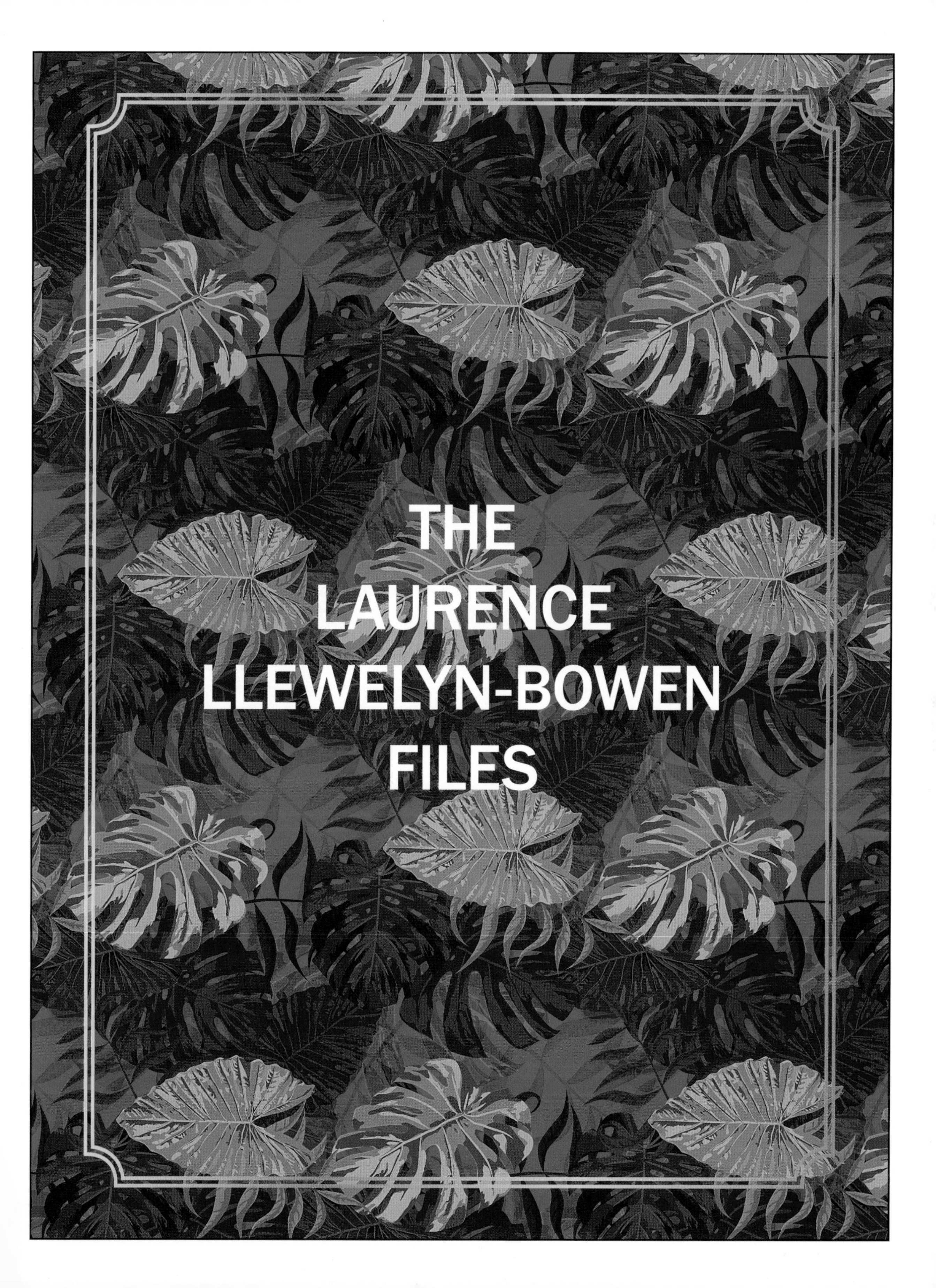
THE
LAURENCE
LLEWELYN-BOWEN
FILES

Date and Time	Location	Additional notes
3rd March 2:15pm	Village – market place 	Came out of the village shop with two bags of food shopping. Noticed he left shopping list in shopping basket, which read 'Buy more cheese and shit'.
15th May 11:37am Laurence	Outskirts of village – Hill View Crescent 	He was on the pavement talking to old man about something – I suspect the weather, as he shook his head at the drizzle. After they finished talking, he walked in direction of the bakery. Followed him briefly then got distracted by a receipt on the floor that looked like a £5 note. Saw him again and he walk past me. I said 'Hi', he replied, 'Do I know you?'
27th May 7:15pm	Village shop 	Carrying basket in village shop. Inside basket: Sherbet Dip Dab and a lettuce. He's such a mad random bastard.
6th July 8:05pm	Drift Close 	Saw him cycling between Drift Close and Foxes Bank Drive. Two carrier bags on both handles. One bag slipped from handle. He stopped to pick it up. I walked past and said, 'Nice weather', sarcastically, as it was raining. He replied, 'No it's not, it's raining.' I don't think he understands sarcasm.

Date and Time	Location	Additional notes
1st September, 9am	Park Road, near school 	Saw him walking his dog wearing a long black leather jacket like Matrix. They stop at traffic lights and he said to dog, 'No, wait for the green man', as if his dog knows what he's talking about? Nutty bastard.
17th September, 3:18pm	Village Cafe 	Saw him in the cafe. He said to waitress, 'Ooh, have you got any of those biscuity thingys?' She said, 'The ones that come on the saucer with the tea?' He said, 'Yes those ones.' She said, 'I'll bring you over a couple.' He said, 'Thanks'. Hate the way he thinks he's entitled to more biscuity thingys cos he's off the telly.
4th October, 12:56pm	Park 	Saw him run after a woman pushing a pram, whilst manically waving a baby's toy that she dropped. He ran so fast his leather jacket was flapping in the wind. I thought he was going to take off. Took him few minutes to catch breath then wondered off in direction of allotments.
18th October, 2pm	Coxwell Street 	Saw him poking around in a skip outside a house. After few minutes he pulled out a piece of MDF. 'Fallen on hard times?' said Kurtan as a joke as we passed him. He replied, 'Fuck off, peasant' under his breath. Kurtan really upset.

LEN

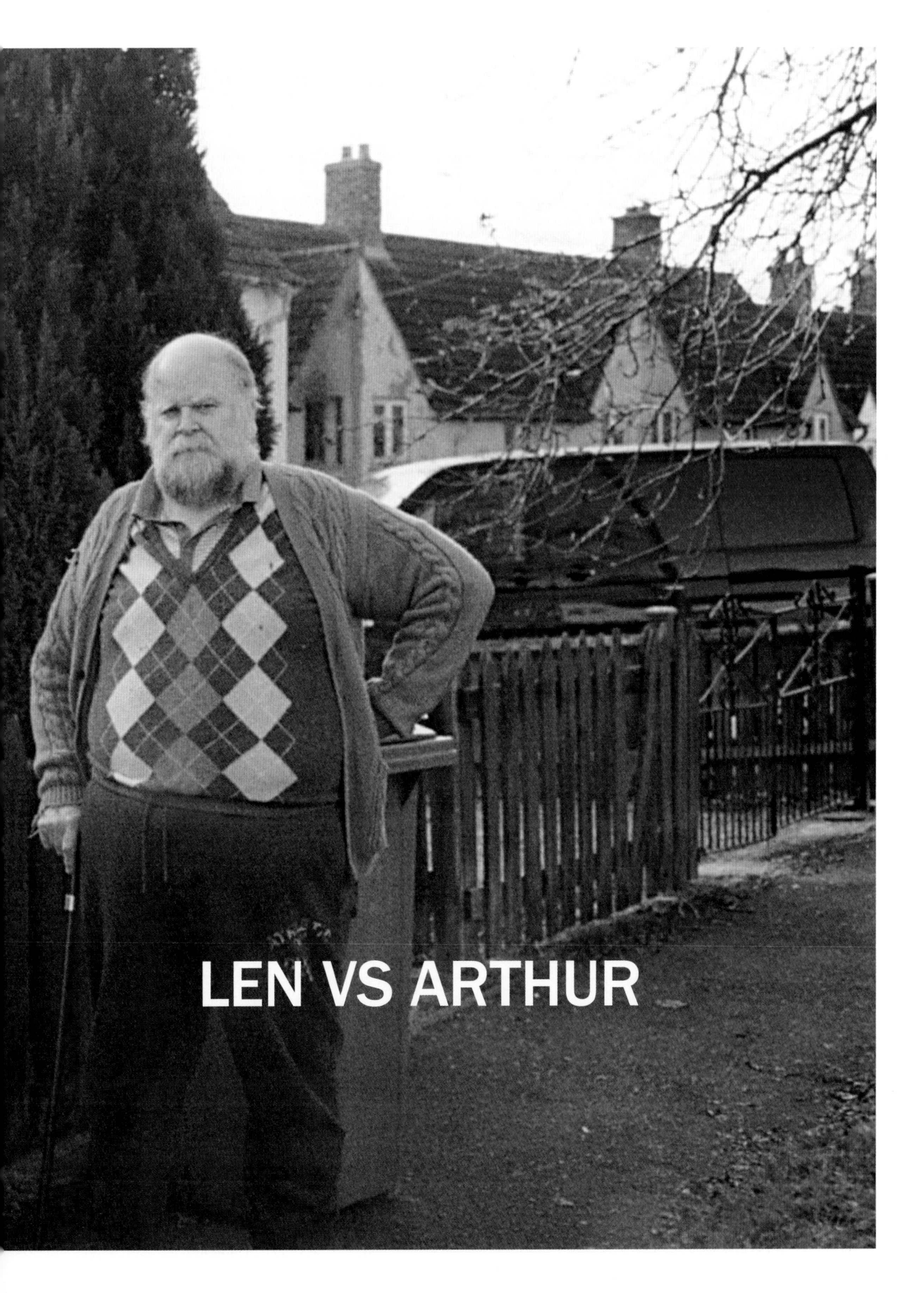

LEN VS ARTHUR

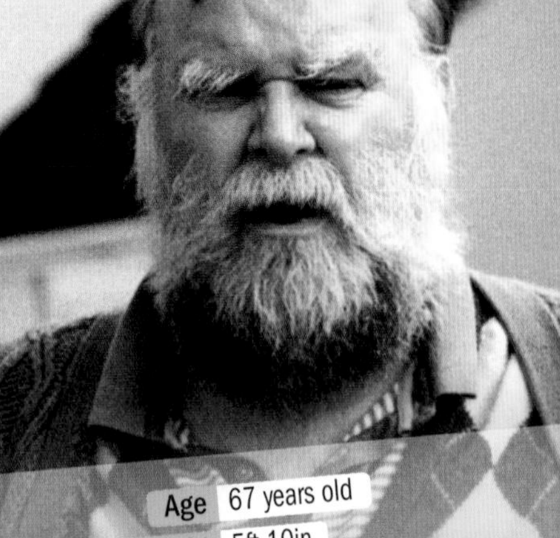

Age	67 years old
Height	5ft 10in
Job	Retired former unemployed
Strengths	Aggression, identifying types of bird, complaining
Weaknesses	Getting involved in everyone's business, pace, everyone he loves dies
Likes	Hoarding, sitting in the window at Bowls Club, Cornflakes
Dislikes	Kerry, Kurtan, Arthur
Favoured Weapon	Brick
Finishing Move	Urinating through your letter box

ARTHUR

Age	83 years old
Height	6ft
Job	Retired former gardener
Strengths	Aggression, collecting vouchers, recycling
Weaknesses	Chronic stomach pain
Likes	Bowls, arguing, circling programmes in the *Radio Times*
Dislikes	Len, old school mate from Australia
Favoured Weapon	Walking stick
Finishing Move	Calling the council

Dear Arthur,
Be aware that recycling bin with L-E-N on it spells LEN not ARTHUR. so please DON'T move from outside MY house and put it outside YOUR house.
Regards
Len

Len,
How dare you say I moved YOUR recycling bin.
I have my OWN recycling bin that I keep chained to a drain pipe outside MY house
Regards Arthur
PS - stop leaving dirty sofas outside YOUR front garden. It makes the street look like a DUMP.

Dear miserable old git,
I seen you eying up MY bin ever since YOU moved into this bloody road. AND DON'T LIE!!
Funny how MY bin ends up outside YOUR house all the time yet you have bin chained up to drainpipe HAHAHA
Regards
Len

Len,

Who you calling miserable old git???
I seen rats run out of your cat flap.
How you like it if I call council?
Get you kicked out once and for all.
Now who's laughing? Not you. ME.
Im laughing. Laughin all the way to the council.

Regards Arthur

Dear Arthur,

You stupid or WHAT?! You move YOUR car. Car blocking MY house. I call council. Then you have no car HAHAHA

Len

Len,

Spoke to council about car. Council fine bout car. Council NOT fine bout SOFA.

Arthur

Arthur,

Funny that. Council nowt said nothin to me bout sofa. But they are livid about YOUR windchimes in garden. FAR TOO LOUD. Keeps whole road awake. chime chime chime 4am 5am 6am. YOU LUCKY WINDCHIME NOT SHOVED UP ~~WHRE~~ SUN DON'T SHINE

Len

Len,

Windchime perfectly allowed. Sofa NOT allowed. Been on phone to council. They are not happy bout sofa. If sofa not gone council are coming. I promise you.

Arthur

Arthur,

Spoke to council bout sofa. Council said 'what sofa???' why you lying to me ARTHUR?? liar liar pants on fire

Len

Len,

I aint liar liar pants on fire. I been speaking to LINDA at council who works at council. If you don't believe me go council and ask for linda. HAHAHA. can't wait to see look on your face when you go council and ask for Linda.

Arthur

THE VILLAGE
TWAT LIST
by Kerry Mucklowe

For those of you unfamiliar with the village I think it's important for me to let you know of some of the biggest twats that populate this shithole. Some are twatier than others and others less twatty than the bigger twats. So here are the biggest twats in the village (in no particular order of twatness). Please note I have removed Len last minute from the Twat List as he fell over in the market place yesterday and it made me feel bad (he's still a twat though).

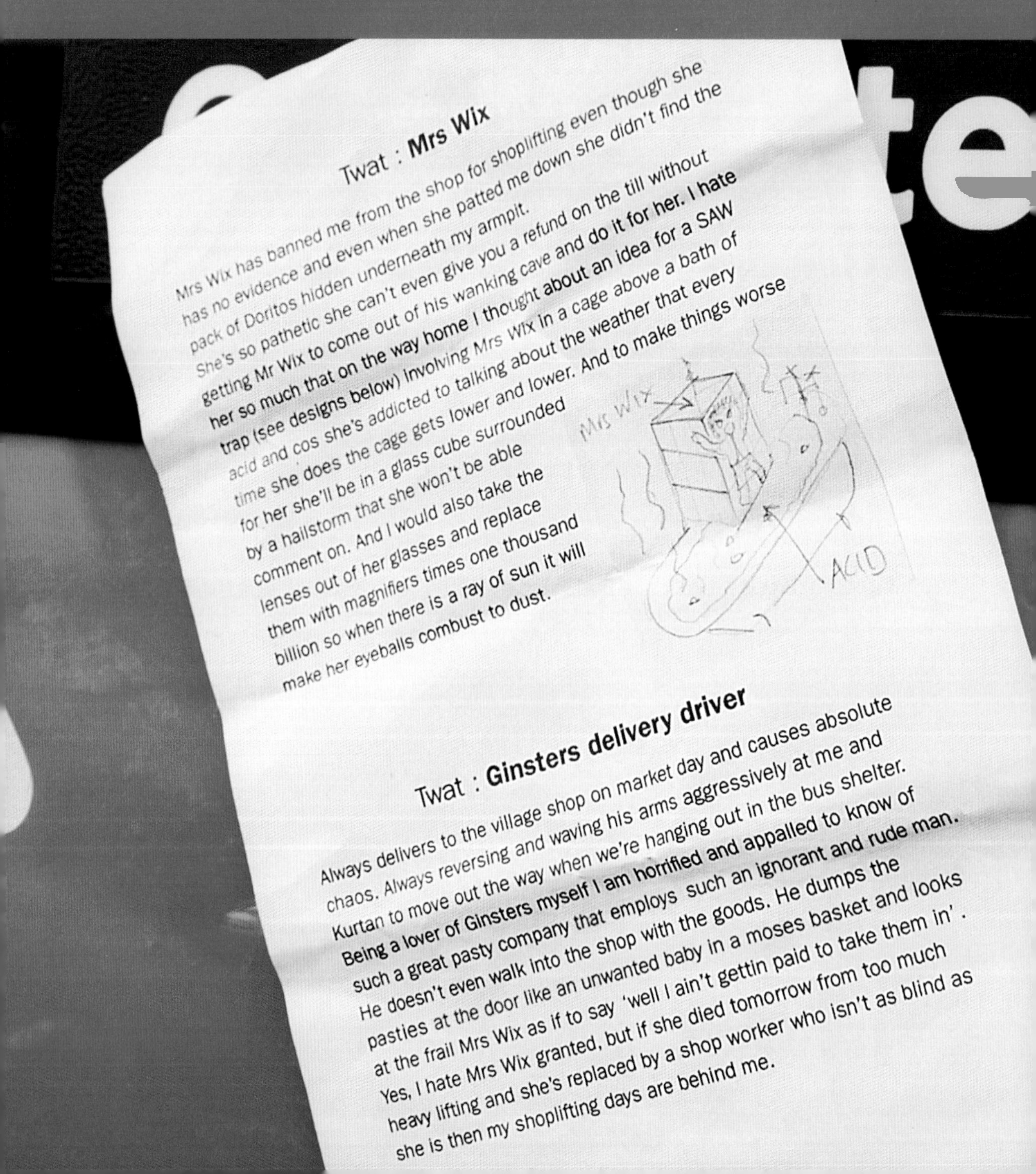

Twat : **Mrs Wix**

Mrs Wix has banned me from the shop for shoplifting even though she has no evidence and even when she patted me down she didn't find the pack of Doritos hidden underneath my armpit.
She's so pathetic she can't even give you a refund on the till without getting Mr Wix to come out of his wanking cave and do it for her. I hate her so much that on the way home I thought about an idea for a SAW trap (see designs below) involving Mrs Wix in a cage above a bath of acid and cos she's addicted to talking about the weather that every time she does the cage gets lower and lower. And to make things worse for her she'll be in a glass cube surrounded by a hailstorm that she won't be able comment on. And I would also take the lenses out of her glasses and replace them with magnifiers times one thousand billion so when there is a ray of sun it will make her eyeballs combust to dust.

Twat : **Ginsters delivery driver**

Always delivers to the village shop on market day and causes absolute chaos. Always reversing and waving his arms aggressively at me and Kurtan to move out the way when we're hanging out in the bus shelter. Being a lover of Ginsters myself I am horrified and appalled to know of such a great pasty company that employs such an ignorant and rude man. He doesn't even walk into the shop with the goods. He dumps the pasties at the door like an unwanted baby in a moses basket and looks at the frail Mrs Wix as if to say 'well I ain't gettin paid to take them in'. Yes, I hate Mrs Wix granted, but if she died tomorrow from too much heavy lifting and she's replaced by a shop worker who isn't as blind as she is then my shoplifting days are behind me.

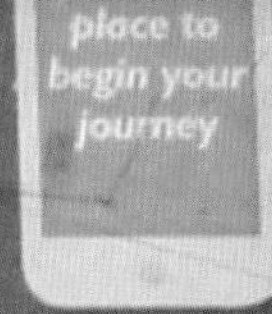

Twat : **Bus driver of the 51 bus**

Huge huge twat. Kurtan hates him cos he sexts his nan. Kurtan showed me some of the messages once and they were absolute filth. He's absolutely obsessed with 'ass play'. Every time he drives past Kurtan's nan in the village he shows off to her by doing hand-brake turns in his bus. He's been the driver of the 51 bus since I can remember and he's a nasty piece of work. He gets a kick out of making everyone stand out in the freezing rain while he finishes the last tokes of his fag. Always loses his shit if you don't have the correct change. He's rude and nasty to the OAPs too. I actually once saw him throw an old man off the bus for dropping a Fisherman's Friend on the floor which rolled down to the pedals. Kurtan wrote a letter to the bus company to complain about him a few years ago without knowing he actually owns the bus company and he replied saying 'hahahahaha fuck you' and now every time he drives past Kurtan's house every quarter past the hour he holds his hand down on the horn continuously. He famously made the papers once for buying a carton of eggs from Sainsbury's and one of them hatched.

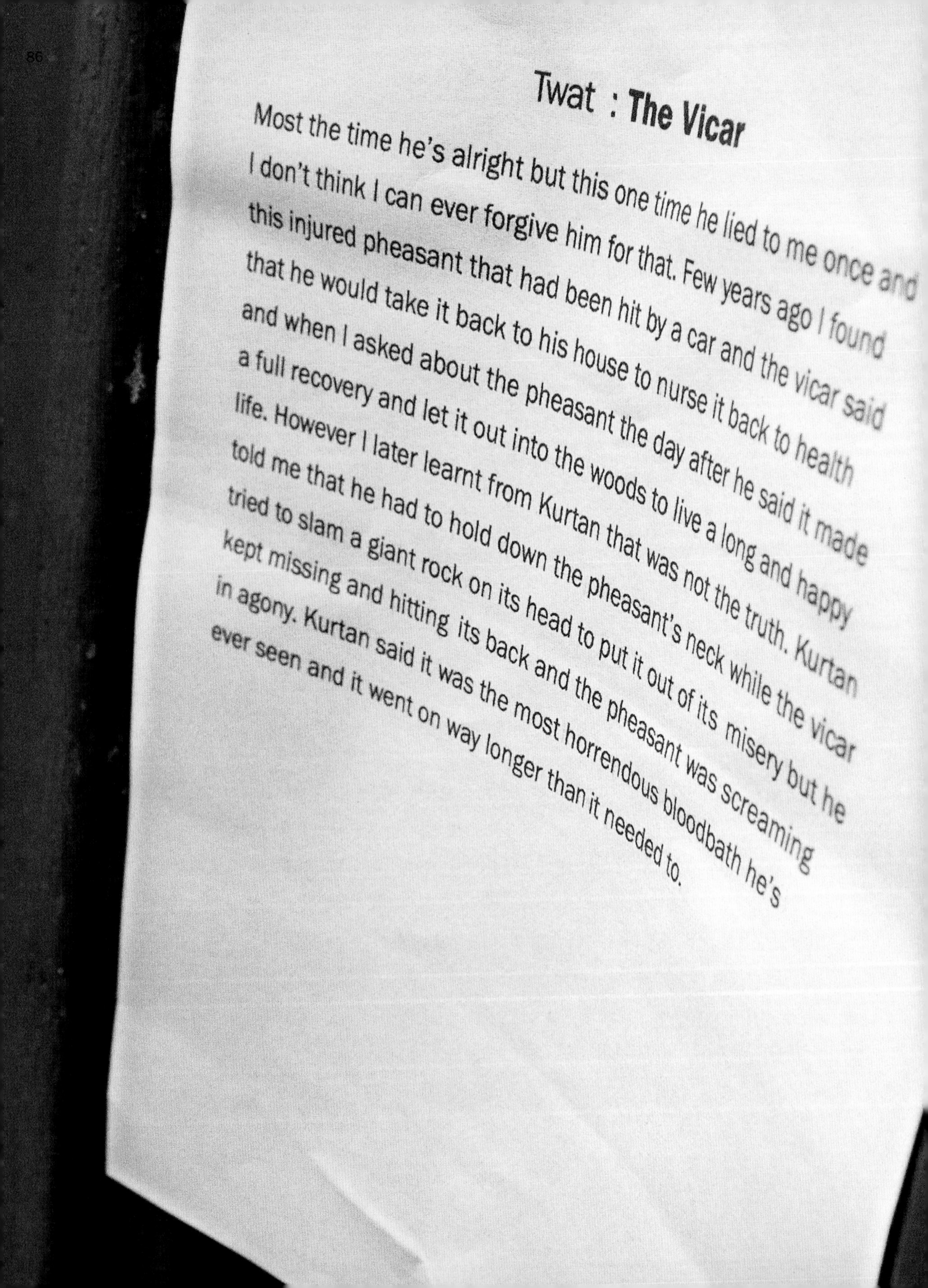

Twat : The Vicar

Most the time he's alright but this one time he lied to me once and I don't think I can ever forgive him for that. Few years ago I found this injured pheasant that had been hit by a car and the vicar said that he would take it back to his house to nurse it back to health and when I asked about the pheasant the day after he said it made a full recovery and let it out into the woods to live a long and happy life. However I later learnt from Kurtan that was not the truth. Kurtan told me that he had to hold down the pheasant's neck while the vicar tried to slam a giant rock on its head to put it out of its misery but he kept missing and hitting its back and the pheasant was screaming in agony. Kurtan said it was the most horrendous bloodbath he's ever seen and it went on way longer than it needed to.

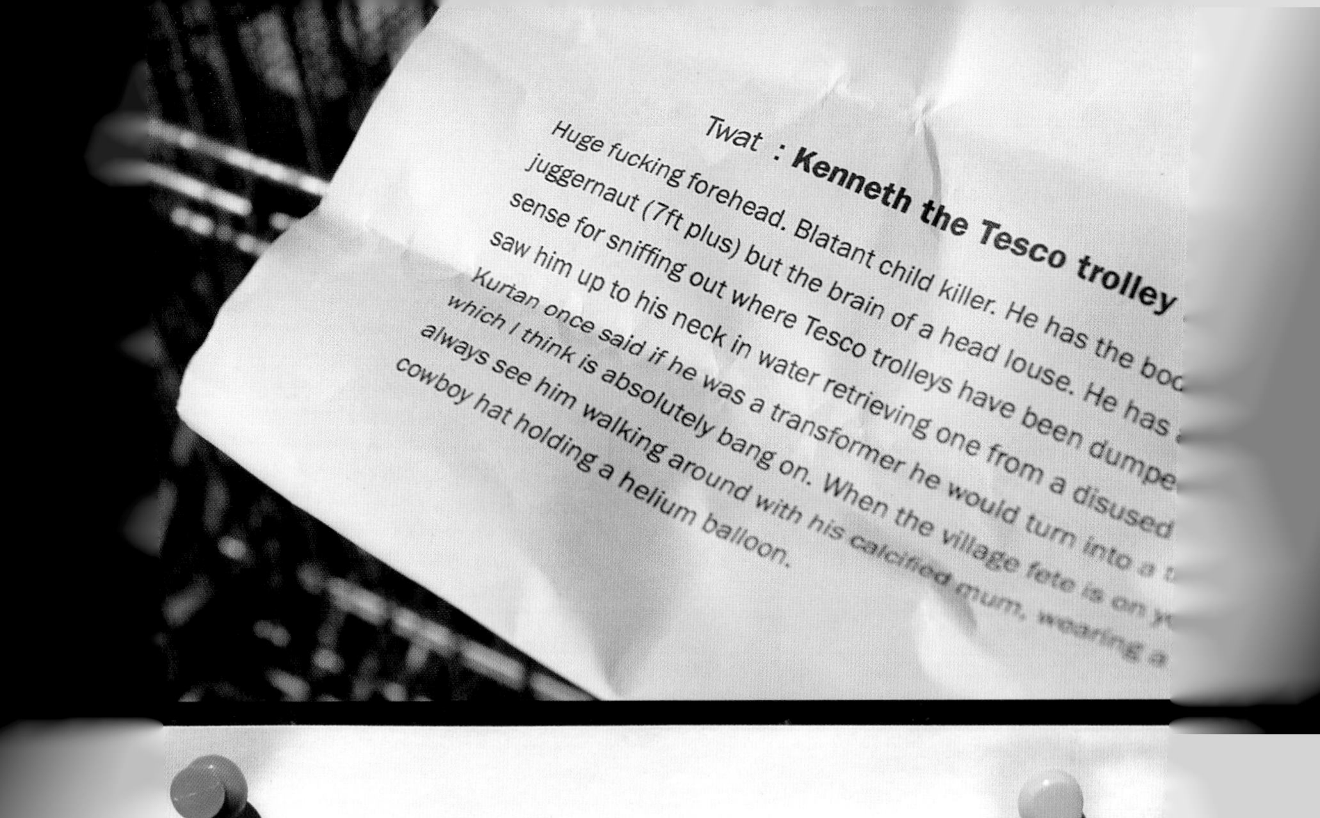
Twat : **Kenneth the Tesco trolley**

Huge fucking forehead. Blatant child killer. He has the bod
juggernaut (7ft plus) but the brain of a head louse. He has
sense for sniffing out where Tesco trolleys have been dumpe
saw him up to his neck in water retrieving one from a disused
Kurtan once said if he was a transformer he would turn into a
which I think is absolutely bang on. When the village fete is on
always see him walking around with his calcified mum, wearing a
cowboy hat holding a helium balloon.

Twat : **Tyson (Mandy's dog)**

Even for a dog he's a massive twat, mainly cos he'll eat anything and then barf it back up again in a matter of seconds. I've seen him barf up a whole hedgehog whose spines had all been dissolved by his stomach acid. Amazingly the hedgehog survived the ordeal but unfortunately two days afterwards made the lethal mistake of building his nest underneath the village bonfire.

Twat : **June**

Busybody. Always telling people to ssshh. Massive gossiper. Shit dress sense. Opened up her garden to the public last summer and had the nerve to charge people 50p entry. As if her garden is even that good?! She'd make more money opening up her pubes to the public. Having said that, I once saw June's pubes at the outdoor swimming pool when she dropped her towel in the changing rooms and if you think her garden is unkempt you should see her thatch. It was like Gandalf's eyebrows – wild, white and thinning.

Twat : **The loud sneezing man**

I don't know his name but he wears a long grey trench coat that is the same colour of his skin. It's so old the buttons have all rusted away. His mouth is always open and he has a face on him like you've just hit him with the most confusing, life changing news. Like this one time I asked him in the cafe if the seat next to him was free and he looked at me as if I told him the year was 3087 and we were ruled by a large lizard alien called Leptor and it's customary to wear pants on your head. He walks at a 45 degree angle as if he's constantly peering over the side of a cliff in a strong wind looking for a lost glove. He's an old man, I guess about 75 and has the loudest most unbelievable sneeze I have ever heard. It's so loud that everyone in the village looks up to the sky and is confused to why they're not seeing an asteroid heading towards the earth. The sound rings through you like a loud YouTube advert before you can turn down the volume. I've genuinely seen pigeons scatter and waitresses drop their trays because of it. And when he's sneezed he carries on staring vacantly into space like nothing has happened. He doesn't even titter when the occasional person says 'bless you'. The man's a lunatic.

Twat : **Colin**

He's an absolute weed. Literally fly paper for bullies. Even the vicar gives him a good old-fashioned ribbing on the bowls green. Bullying Colin isn't even satisfying any more. It's so easy. Some of the things we call him are Lightbulb Head, High Trousers, Mr Sheen, Girl-wrists, Safari Shirt, Casio Cock (in reference to his watch), Stalk Legs, Golf Socks, Wart Thumb, Mr Smiley, DJ Sneakers, Butter Fingers, Pot Noodle for One, Gollum, Charlie Brown and the Peanut Brain, Mr Bean, Chinless Wonder, Mini Egg Speckled Head and Internet Explorer (cos he takes ages to react). He's often seen at the Bowls Club despite being shit at bowls and constantly letting his team down. Otherwise you'll see him on the computers at the library searching for old school chums on Friends Reunited like the sad twat he is.

Twat : **Councillor Andrews**

Posh turd. Hates me and Kurtan. Once named and shamed me. Manipulates the vicar.

Twat : **Farmer Jenkins**

Odd man. Keeps himself to himself. Smelliest man in the village hands down. Manages to out-stink Len by a thousand (considering Len smells like fish fingers left out in the sun). Pig farmer by trade, his wax jacket must absorb the smell of pig shite like a sponge. If I'm in the village shop I can literally smell him approaching 2 minutes before he comes in. He's like a Glade plug-in filling the room with his scent of boiled faggots, cowpat fondue and damp soggy sheep dogs who still have cling-ons attached to the fur on their asses. When he walks into the village you can see a long trail of mud and grass behind him. He could walk a thousand miles and still there would be chunks of mud flying from his boots. He's like the pied piper for flies. Kurtan once typed the address of Jenkins' farm into Google Earth and is convinced he can see Jenkins shoving his cock and bollocks in the exhaust pipe of his tractor.

Twat : **Dog in pram around village**

Another dog makes my Twat List and for a very good reason. He's a small dog, I suspect an elderly one cos his tongue is always hanging out the side of his mouth cos his teeth have rotted away. But that's not the reason why he's a twat, the reason why he's a twat is that he gets pushed around in a pushchair and is almost famous in the village for it. It's become a travelling freak show. And as a joke the owner stuck an 'L' plate on the back of the pram which I don't find funny at all, I think it's social suicide for both the owner and the dog. It's not even like the dog can't walk, he CAN walk but chooses not to cos he thinks he's better than everyone. To be honest I think he's been raised to believe he is above human beings which is a really bad attitude to have in life as a dog. The dog always has his nose high up in the air too as if it's directing the pram with its thoughts. I cannot wait to see the look on his face when he bounces off the front of the 51 bus when his owner carelessly parades him into the middle of the road. They even let him in the Post Office which shows no respect for the 'guide dogs only' sign on the door.

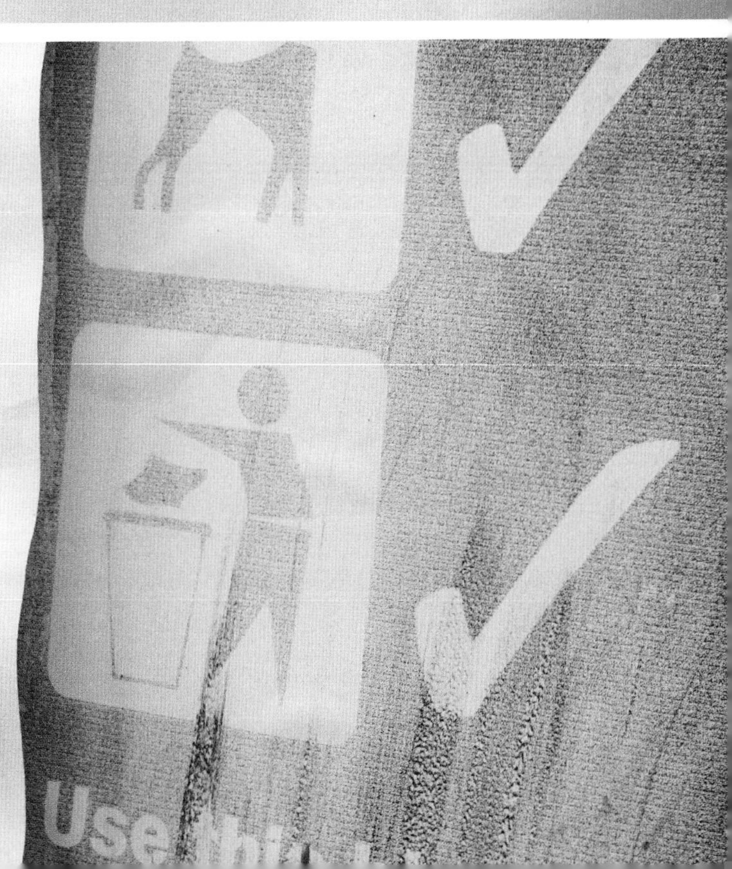

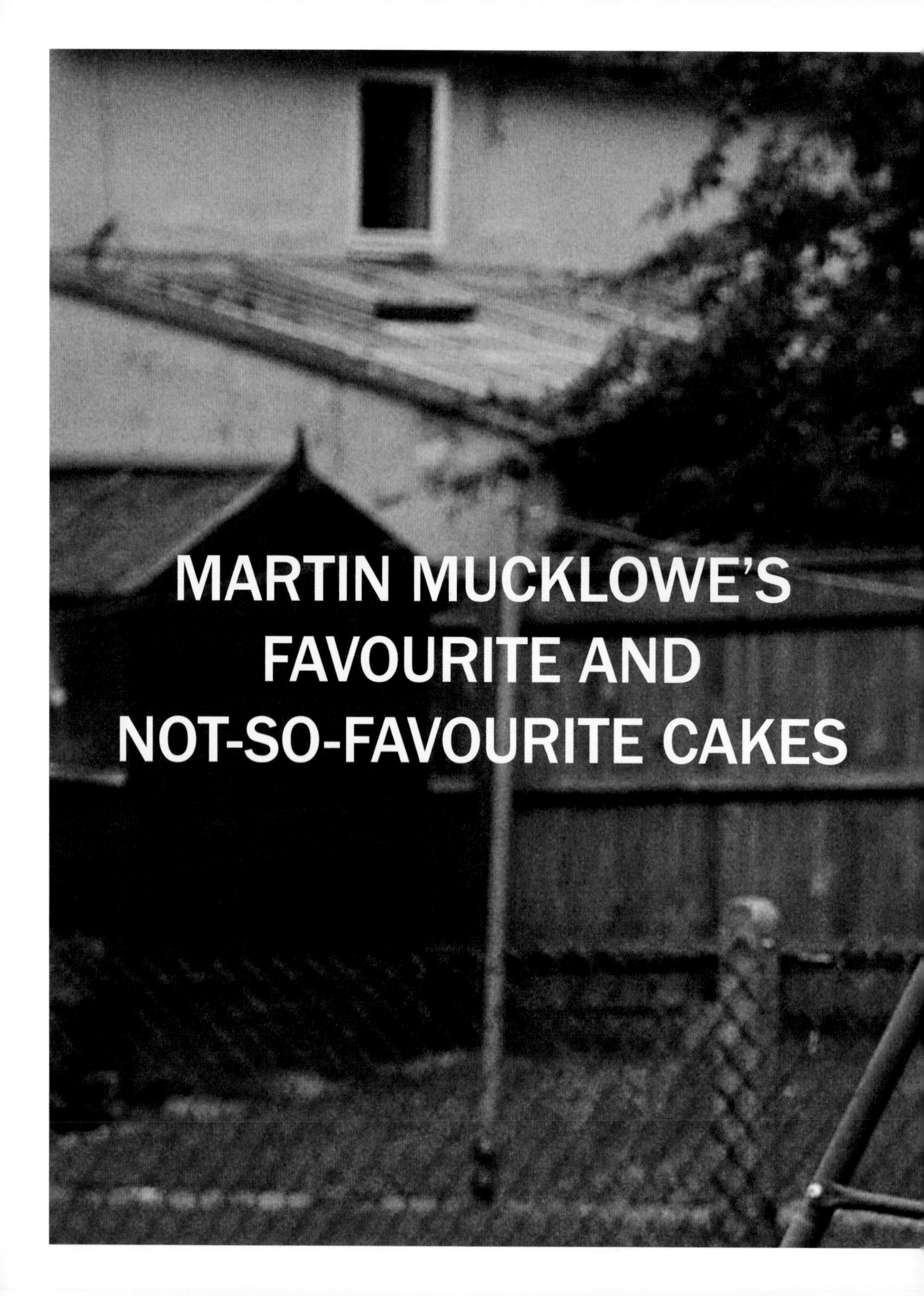

MARTIN MUCKLOWE'S FAVOURITE AND NOT-SO-FAVOURITE CAKES

My Favourite and Not-so-Favourite Cakes

Baking is a passion of mine, second behind women. Cakes are a lot like women, actually. Some can be sweet and moist, others dry and bottom-heavy. It can be a bloody minefield out there, so here's my definitive list of my favourite and not-so-favourite cakes.

Butterfly Cake

Also called Fairy Cake, but I've got a reputation to think of. Such a delicate little cake that is named thus because of its delicate wings. The sponge mix is so aerated it wafts down your throat like a cloud. I get quite emotional baking this marvellous cake and I ain't ashamed to admit it. If the lightness of a cake never brought you to tears, then you ain't a proper man, in my opinion. I wouldn't take this to work, as Dan and that wouldn't understand the subtleties of this gentle offering.

Dundee Cake

If I was on a desert island and only allowed one cake, it would always be the trusty Dundee Cake. It shouts fruit, spice and nuts with every mouthful, like getting a treble 20 on the darts with every throw. When I am in the mood, I spread some salted butter on a slice to give it that extra richness. I'm glad that bloody Hadrian's Wall was pulled down so this wonderful offering could be treasured down South. Dundee is also the name of my favourite crocodile poacher, which makes it that extra special.

Black Forest Gateau

There is only one place for this German pudding and that is in the bin or at the circus, to chuck into a clown's face.

Brownie

American concoction that – like the grey squirrel and the American crayfish – is trying to take over our beloved isle. Stick it where the sun don't shine – it's the same bloody colour after all!

Upside-Down Cake

Make it the right way up in the first place, FFS.

Sponge Cake

When I comes across someone who thinks they know more about baking than me, I just say to them, 'Flour, sugar, eggs; Flour, sugar, eggs'. Like a mantra. Baking at its most simple, and at the same time at its most difficult. I often say, 'Let's bake here and now and see who's best.' When they give me their offering, I break it in half. On one half I do the crumble test, crumbling it in my right hand. If the consistency is not right, I laugh in their face and throw the other half as far as I can.

Battenberg

It's all about the symmetry with this one. You should be able to slice it and then lay the slices together and have a game of chess on it. Some people think it's a German cake, but they are wrong cos it's as British as a good vindaloo.

Red Velvet Cake

Another poncy offering from the other side of the Atlantic. Trendy types buy the shop version, and, as my old man used to say when Mum came in after a night out shagging GIs during the war, 'GO HOME YANKS!'

Victoria Sponge

The most regal and British of cakes. Named after Her Majesty Queen Victoria, who was very much like me – loved a slice and a shag. But if there is one cake that makes me mad, it's this one, because some bastards try to cut corners or make subtle changes. NO! Make it the traditional way.

1. Raspberry jam and vanilla cream as the filling NOT whipped cream. It ain't a school dinner jelly!
2. A dusting of icing sugar NOT caster sugar. I want to be able to roll up a 10-pound note and snort it without losing me septum.
3. Always, and I repeat, ALWAYS serve it on your finest china. If you're gonna come at me with it on a paper plate, I'll punch it back in your face. If you don't respect the cake, how do you expect me to respect you??

Faworki

I had a Polish lad who used to work for me on the building site by the name of Jakub. Bloody good worker to be fair, we couldn't keep up with him. On Cake Tuesday he would present this sweet crisp cake in the shape of a bow. Me and Dan burst out laughing and took the right royal piss. Then I tasted it and humbly bent down by his feet and wept.

Hash Brownie

Also called 'Space Cakes', made with weed.
Typical Dutch, always off their faces. No wonder they only came in a disappointing second to us in ruling the high seas. In the past, I have made a legal version of the Hash Brownie called the Amber Leaf Brownie. It didn't quite meet expectations, to be honest with you.

Jaffa Cakes

Nuff said.

Lemon Drizzle Cake

One of the new breed. Needs to be fluffy and moist at the same time. Needs to zing when you taste it, like testing a battery out with your tongue.

Angel Cake

Sponge, cream and food colouring. I will leave that to Madam Kipling and his merry band of shop-boughts.

Avocado Cake

Get out of my house now and never darken my door.

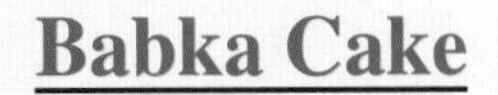

Babka Cake

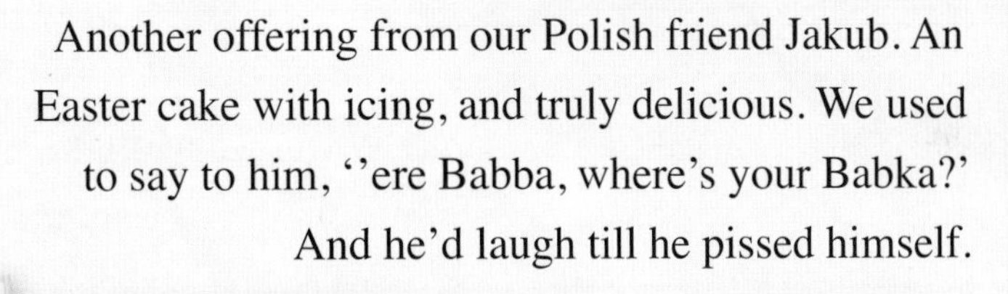

Another offering from our Polish friend Jakub. An Easter cake with icing, and truly delicious. We used to say to him, ''ere Babba, where's your Babka?' And he'd laugh till he pissed himself.

Carrot Cake

I'm really not sure about this. It reminds me of women with hairy legs, wearing dungarees and sweating a lot.

Caterpillar Cake

Classic birthday cake often found in supermarkets such as Tesco. This cake should never be eaten; it's purely just to blow out the candles and for them to dim the lights at Pizza Hut and sing 'Happy Birthday'. If this was based on taste it'd be first in line for the execution chamber, but it's the cheeky little fella's face that never fails to raise a smile. Blow out the candles, chuck it in the bin. Job done.

KURTAN'S BRAIN DUMP

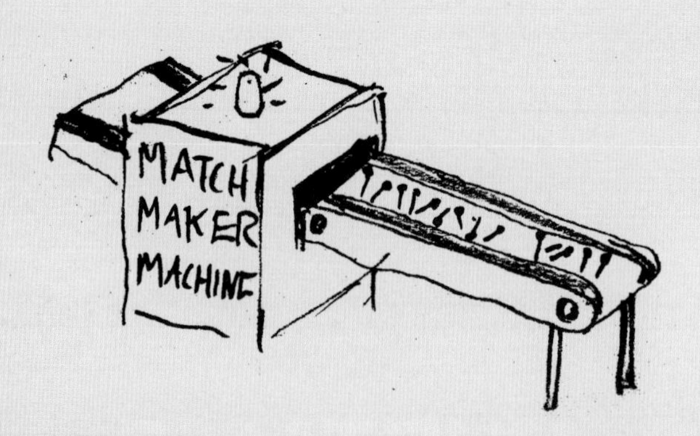

Idea for a film. Thriller/action movie.

Perfect vehicle for Tom Hanks. Tom Hanks living in New York and working this shitty job and basically gets shat on by his boss every day and works his fingers to the bone. One day he is fed up walking home and stumbles into a laboratory where this mad scientist is trying to work out how to make matches without cutting down trees, so he's made a machine that you put a match into and it duplicates the match into thousands of other matches. Tom Hanks basically ends up spilling coffee on the floor by accident and slips into the machine and ends up duplicating himself. At first he's like 'oh shit what have I done' but then he's like 'fuck it, I'll use it to my advantage.' So then he gets his Tom Hanks Clone to go to his work and take shit from his boss while the real Tom Hanks goes to the arcade and plays videogames all day. Then the real Tom Hanks gets a phone call from the mad scientist saying, 'shit mate you need to come back here, I tried to clone ten thousand matches but I accidentally cloned ten thousand Tom Hanks and I don't know what to do with them.' All the Tom Hanks start dispersing and they walk into the roads and cause massive pileups on the motorways etc. The army gets involved and basically starts wiping out all the Tom Hanks by dropping grenades and smoke bombs on them. The real Tom Hanks has to prove to the army that he's the real Tom Hanks by telling his family things only the real Tom Hanks would know. In the end his family and the army believe him and wipe out all the Tom Hank clones. Then BIG TWIST – the mad scientist says to the army they killed the wrong Tom Hanks and the only Tom Hanks still alive is actually a clone so the Tom Hanks that you think is real the whole time is actually a clone. SECOND BIG TWIST – Tom Hanks wakes up and it's all a dream. THIRD BIG TWIST – It's not the real Tom Hanks, it's a clone. The film is called 'Will the Real Tom Hanks Please Stand Up'.

'On the Run' staring Matt Damon

Idea for a film called 'On the Run' staring Matt Damon who is an FBI cop and wakes up on his honeymoon to find his wife dead next to him. Everyone accuses him of doing it so he goes on the run trying to find out who murdered his wife and at the same time not getting caught by the FBI. In the end he finds out it actually was him but can't really remember cos he blacked out. And when he goes to hand himself in to the police he sees his wife out the window driving around in a new Lamborghini with his old best school friend (Matt Le Blanc) who throughout the whole film is the only one who believes him and helps him hide etc WHICH IS WHY THIS IS SO SHOCKING AT THE END. Cut to flashbacks of Matt Damon and Matt Le Blanc both at school sat next to each other and the teacher is reading out the register and she says 'Matt?' and they both put their hands up. Then they both laugh. The end.

'Bull in a China Shop'

Idea for a film made by PIXAR called 'Bull in a China Shop'. Basically a bull gets employed by a china shop and everything goes wrong. A woman comes into the shop to browse and pulls out a red hanky to blow her nose. This turns the bull's eyes into spirals. And before he knows it his back legs start kicking everything. He starts smashing up all the china just as his boss walks in (voice of Eddie Murphy). The boss says 'that's so typical of you'. The end.

John Lewis advert

Idea for a Christmas John Lewis advert. Basically John Lewis adverts were only invented to A) make people cry and B) make you buy gifts from John Lewis. Over the last few years John Lewis has really dropped the ball. Hopefully this idea will get them back on track and touch the hearts of a nation.

Scene 1 – Basically it's Christmas Day and Father Christmas has just delivered all the presents to all the kids around the world and he's absolutely fucking drained. He walks through the front door and he bangs his head on the door frame (**we hear a comedy sound and canned laughter**). He then walks into the living room and he takes his boots off and he's just about to sit down in front of the TV to watch 'Despicable Me 3' on ITV2 and Mrs Father Christmas is like 'don't think you're sitting down, you just trampled mucky snow all in the carpet' (**canned laughter**)…'You don't ever think do you?! And there's shit loads of letters come through the post from kiddies for next year, so get answering them' and Father Christmas is raging and he goes 'listen right, I'm so fuckin stressed, I've just been round the world 5 times and I've only been back 2 minutes so shut your gob, you don't do anything'…and she goes mad and is like 'get out of my face, get out of my face' with her hand up to his face pushing his face…and basically Father Christmas snaps and says 'what about MY Christmas? All I wanna do is watch "Despicable Me 3" and I ain't seen it yet'…and she just turns round to him and says 'your breath stinks' and this is the final straw…Then Father Christmas walks out to the barn where he grabs his shotgun and he's looking at Rudolf and Rudolf is basically looking back chewing on hay, completely oblivious to the fact that Father Christmas is holding a shotgun to his furry forehead. Then Father Christmas pats him on the head and says, 'good night old faithful' then the camera pans across to the corner of the barn and off-screen we hear this gunshot sound and the camera pans back to reveal Rudolf on the floor with his brains blown out and his

legs still twitching, then Father Christmas slowly turns the gun on himself then **GUNSHOT** - CUT TO: black screen…text on screen:

'Has anyone ever thought about giving Father Christmas a present?'

over black screen we hear the sound of the barn door fling open and Mrs Father Christmas comes in screaming and shouting, 'You silly silly bastard, you silly silly bastard'. Screen turns red with blood. FADE TO BLACK. The end.

Director's note: I think this will definitely get people crying and increase sales of 'Despicable Me 3' tenfold.

theme park

Idea for a theme park based on the 1998 PIXAR film 'A Bug's Life'. Basically there's these huge animatronic boots that go round trying to stamp on everyone and in the cafe all they serve is giant leaves and for cups they have giant acorn husks. And the long walk to the main gates of the park is made to look like a crack in between a pavement.

Don't get the 9 of Clubs

Idea for a card game called 'Don't get the 9 of Clubs'. 2-player game. Rules: Shuffle out the cards between both players and if you get the 9 of Clubs you lose the game. Note to self - copyright this asap.

Blue Peter Tortoise film

Idea for a film. PIXAR? About the Blue Peter tortoise that outlives all the generations of Blue Peter presenters. He lives so old that everyone he loves dies. Bit like the film 'Bicentennial Man' but with a tortoise (voice of Adam Sandler). Young Katie Hill played by Michelle Keegan. Old Katie Hill played by Judie Dench. Scene on Katie Hill's deathbed where she realises that the star of Blue Peter was not the presenters, it was the tortoise all along. Funny scene - tortoise falls down Katie Hill's blouse and he's biting her nipples and the tortoise says 'this is the life'. And Katie Hill says 'he doesn't know any better, he's just a tortoise' and the tortoise says 'that's what you think'. Cue laughter (maybe use this scene for trailer).

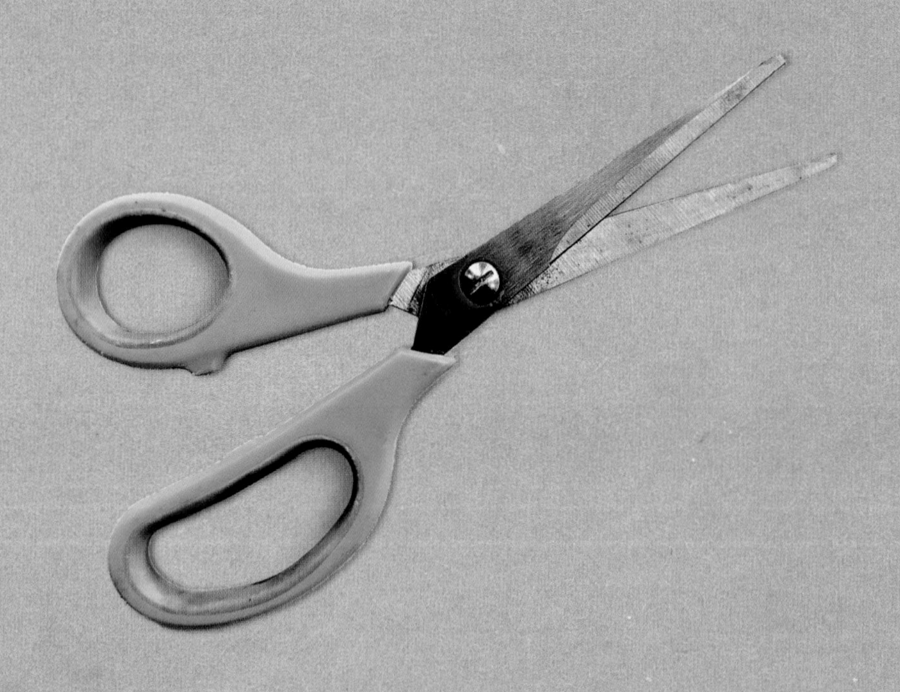

Threatening Letters

Dear Kerry,
I often see you around the village. I have been having intense fantasies about you that I feel I must share with you. My dream is that you come over to mine in your Swindon shirt. You come in to fix my washing machine and you are all sweaty cos you have been playing football in the park. You smell of BO but I don't mind. You are so strong your hands are like spanners. You lift me above your head and throw me to the other side of the room and smash me against the wall. We arm wrestle to ignore the time and when you beat me you tell me how pathetic I am. I give you my belt to whip me with and my trousers fall down and you laugh at my genitals.

Dear Kerry,
I had another fantasy about you last night. You were the South West Bowling Champion and I was working at the local bowling alley as a part-time Saturday boy. You complain that your bowling shoes aren't clean enough so you spray cleaner into my mouth and make me lick your bowling shoes clean. Then you say lane number 9 is short of a bowling pin and you force me to replace it with myself. I stand there for hours while you throw balls at me. Your bowling is so hard and accurate it starts to break my shin bones and they splinter all over the bowling lane. Then you grab me by the ball bag, take me over to the ball polisher machine and shove my balls into it. I'm screaming in agony while you laugh with your friend big Mandy and say 'it's the price you pay for having dirty balls'. When you pull my balls out they have shrunk to the size of marbles. You humiliate me by parading me around the bowling alley and pointing at my marble-sized testicle and saying 'look how smooth and shiny his small testicals are.

Dear Kerry,

I cannot stop fantasizing about you. My latest was the best. I am cleaning out my shed when you come in and tell me you want to sand down a chair leg. So you use my mouth as a vice and tell me I cannot breathe. I breathe involuntarily to stay alive and you punch me in the lungs and tell me how pathetic I am.

Dear Kerry,

I would love to tell you about this fantasy I had where I'm your human lab rat and you are performing experiments on me as you work for the Chinese military to test out the most painful and effective torture methods. You have been told to focus on the pain of the genital area as this has shown really effective in tests. The first experiment is to see how long a man can be dangled by his testicals for until he passes out. I'm dangled from makeshift scaffolding which is chained to my balls and I swing like a pendular clock. You laugh and you write down the results on your clipboard and I can see as I'm swinging what you are writing. You write that I have small testicals and therefore fail the test. In the next experiment you chain me to a ceiling fan with my legs strapped in the splits so just my bollocks are dangling down. Then you turn on the fan and I spin round and round while you and big Mandy swing at my testicals with large baseball bats.

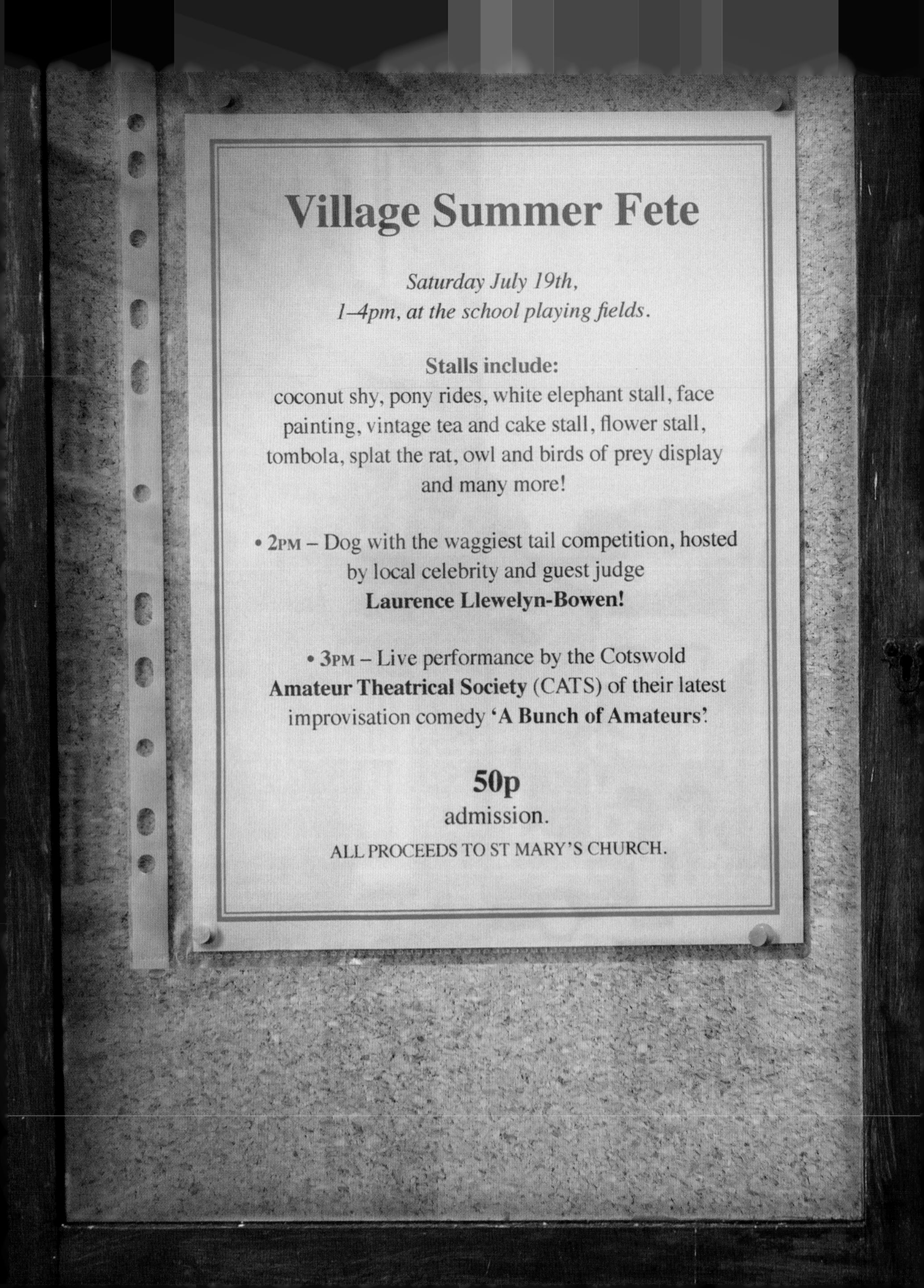

Village Summer Fete

Saturday July 19th,
1–4pm, at the school playing fields.

Stalls include:
coconut shy, pony rides, white elephant stall, face painting, vintage tea and cake stall, flower stall, tombola, splat the rat, owl and birds of prey display and many more!

• **2PM** – Dog with the waggiest tail competition, hosted by local celebrity and guest judge
Laurence Llewelyn-Bowen!

• **3PM** – Live performance by the Cotswold **Amateur Theatrical Society** (CATS) of their latest improvisation comedy **'A Bunch of Amateurs'**.

50p
admission.

ALL PROCEEDS TO ST MARY'S CHURCH.

WANTED:

Seeking information on man called **'Robert Robinson'**.

Last seen in Class 5 at Holly Park School around 2004.

Approach with caution.
Known to hiss at dogs.

Contact Kurtan Mucklowe
urgently on 1223 854093.
Any information gratefully received.

Below is a sketch of what I suspect he might look like now.

NOTICE

PLEASE CAN THE PERSON PUTTING CIGARETTE BUTTS IN THE PLANTERS PLEASE STOP.

Welcome to
Wandsworth
Reform Prison
HM PRISON
SERVICE
H.M.P Wandsworth
No Vehicle Access

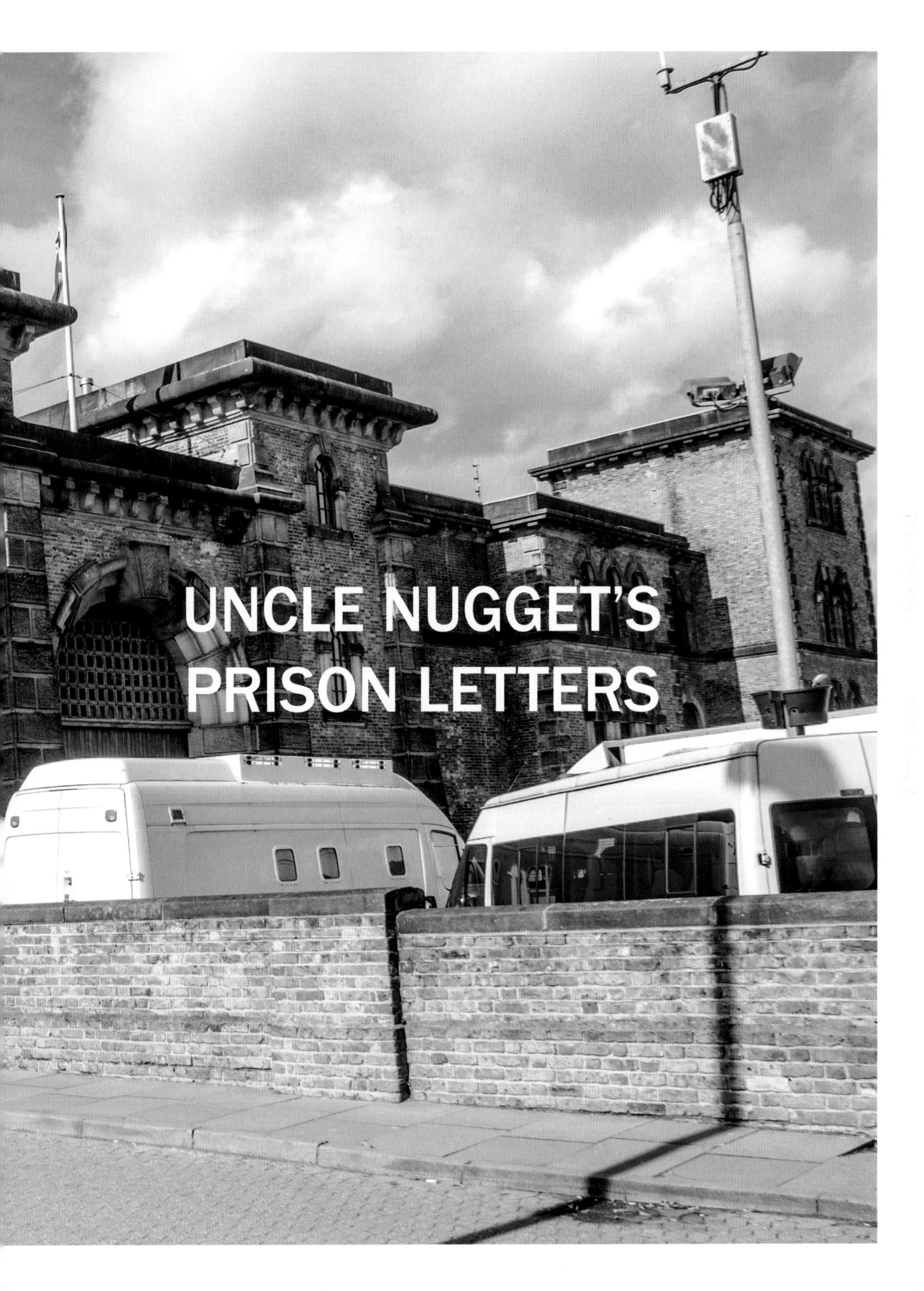

UNCLE NUGGET'S PRISON LETTERS

HM PRISON
SERVICE

19th July 2018

Dear Kerry and Kurtan,
Thank you very much for your letter regarding not being able to send any more letters. It was a joke obviously? I chuckled to myself all nite about that so thanks for that. You two jokers!!
I have been very well. Yesterday we had prison bake-off. I baked some cheese scones with the help of my cell-mate Knives. He put too much cheese in em which fucking ruined em. Cheese burnt all on the baking tray, was so fucking livid I burst into tears. Me and Knives ended up having a bit of a tiff and I accidentally cracked his head open on the stove. Unfortunately I shall be no longer allowed to participate in the prison bake-off. Knives is fine by the way, but due to his head injury cant remember his birthdate or recognise himself in the mirror which is probably a good thing coz he's an ugly bastard. My prison officer Wendy has encouraged me to take up knitting.
Do you know any birds that can write to me, only interested in ones with massive jugs FF plus.
Or just a poster/doodle of one is fine.
Much love from your favourite Uncle
Nugget x

HM PRISON
SERVICE

23rd July 2018

Dear Kerry and Kurtan,

Haven't received a reply to my last letter which is a bit annoying. I assume it got lost in the post??

This week I learnt to count to 10. I get a bit stuck after the number 7 but as soon as I get to 9 I'm absolutely sailing through it then. I'm currently writing a novel about how the government is spying on us via CCTV. As discussed, is there any way you can send me a poster of a girl with big jugs? Also my mate Knives says hi. Is it possible he can stay with you when he comes out? You may have to tie him up with dog chains at night as he accidentally goes round murdering people in his sleep, but during the day he's as sound as can be, as long as you don't let him near your cheese scones teehee teehee

By the way, it's visiting hours on Thursday. I assume you're both coming in to see me? So excited to show you off to my cellmates. I showed a picture of you Kurtan to my mate big Don and he thinks you're really sexy and wants to know if you fancy a coffee sometime? He does have a wife but prison does a funny thing to yer. Also I can't wait for you to meet my pet fly Albus.

All the best

Uncle Nugget

PS my reflection started talking to me last night, but that's a story I'll save till I see ya! Lol.

HM PRISON
SERVICE

1st August 2018

Dear Kerry and Kurtan,

VERY UPSET you did not come and visit me Thursday.
I WAITED AND WAITED and you
NEVER SHOWED UP??
If you died in a bus accident on the way here,
I am considering forgiving yer. But if not WHERE
WERE YOU???
Even Knives dad came in to visit him,
and he hasn't been speaking to him since Knives set
him on fire with a petrol bomb.
My reflection said you didn't come because you both
don't really like me and he was trying to get me to stab
you both but I told him to chill out a bit. Fortunately
me and Knives are both out tomorrow so we shall
come straight round yours. We shall probably even be there
before this letter gets to you! Teehee. Looking forward
to seeing my favourite niece and nephew and assassinating
the prime minister. Also, I learnt how to make my own
bookmarks by cutting up Cornflakes boxes. I can
show you if you want.

Love your favourite Uncle,
Nugget

Gloucestershire Constabulary **CRIME REPORT**

Reporting Officer:	PC Webber	Badge Number:	0372
Date of Crime:	5/02/2018	Crime Ref:	GC/0621/SN

Incident: Threats to destroy or damage property,
Possession of offensive weapon in a public place.

Details of Event:

On Thursday, 3rd September, 2016, at approximately 17:59 hours, I responded to a call from Mrs Sarah Wilkins reporting a disturbance at Tesco Metro store, 4 Market Place, Fairford. Upon my arrival, I observed the suspect Steve Nuggins, bare-chested, wielding a blade (a 73cm-long samurai sword) above his head whilst repeating the sentence 'I shouldn't be doing this.' I approached the suspect with caution and asked him to place the blade on the ground, which he did. I proceeded to handcuff the suspect who was very co-operative until he was refused a portable DVD player in his cell so he could watch episodes of 'Friends'. After attempting to assault PC Gilbey, the suspect was restrained but was later calmed down when PC Gilbey allowed him to quote funny lines from the show. When questioned on his public disturbance, Steve Nuggins replied, 'I was only having a laugh.'

'ME LIFE'

by Sue Mucklowe
(Kerry's mum)

'Me Life'

by Sue Mucklowe
(Kerry's mum)

I lived in the village all me life. I got 5 sisters and 1 brothers. Me dad was a farmer and on the side would brew his own moonshine that he sold out the back of his cart and me mother was a truffle snuffler. Most people used domesticated pigs, 'truffle hogs' they call em, to be able to snuffle out truffles, but god blessed me dear mum with a special gift for sniffing em out herself. She'd go out on the land on all fours, rootin around in some undergrowth and dig em out with her bare hands. She'd give them to me dad who'd take them em up to Derby Fair and sell them to restaurant owners for a shilling and tuppence a-piece.

One day me old mum went out on the snuffle and never came back

One day me old mum went out on the snuffle and never came back. All me dad found was a note left on the kitchen table sayin 'met someone, off to London'. So me old pa travelled all the way to London on the back of a sheep herd. It took him 5 days and when he returned he told us that she had run away and shacked up with some young Italian pot wash called Dolmio, who promised her romance and a wonderful life or whatnot. He went on to become a successful pasta sauce maker. Years later we found out she didn't have a good life. Dolmio was a cruel man and would strap her to the bike rack on the top of his motor and travel round Europe with her on a leash making her snuffle out truffles in return for a bucket of offal. Me dad was heartbroken and he never fully recovered from that. He didn't know how to wash his trousers or cook his dinner. He was a shell of himself. Me and me sisters did it for him. We'd cook him livers on a Mondays, stuffed hearts on a Tuesdays, Wednesdays was trotters, Thursdays sheeps tongues and Fridays spag bol. Saturdays brains, Sundays leftover brains.

Dating was a lot different back in my day, none of this Tinder or whatnot. On me 18th birthday me dad poked me out of bed with his pitchfork and said, 'c'mon get out of bed you old girl, put some lippy on and your best frock, we're gonna find you a fella to wed who can help me out on the farm.' That morning he marched me down to the local cattle market where there were twenty or so young farmhands from the village lined up against the troughs. Me dad would walk up and down the line inspectin them, pokin them with his stick, shining a torch in their mouths and giving em a hard punch in the diaphragm. When me dad thought he found a suitable suitor he'd tap em on the shoulder, the fella would come forward and they would take their top off and wrestle, and if they managed to pin down me old dad they secured me hand in marriage and their hand on the farm.

They would meet up in the barn at night and wrestle until the early hours of the morn

Many tried, many failed, except for one young chap called Simple John. He was tall and strong but had the mind of a child. Me dad was happy cos John was a marvellous sheep whisperer. He'd whisper in their ears and they would pass out and he'd stack em up on his cart like breeze blocks and transport them to the barn for shaving. Weddings weren't such a big thing like nowadays. It was a simple service, no nice frock nor nothin, just me, John and me dad on the farm in front of the pigs, me father called the vicar out, we said our vows and that was that. Gettin on with it like. And as soon as it were over we got back to work muckin out the cows. I liked John but he was terrible shy in the bedroom department and even on our wedding night we never did the deed. He took quite a shine to me brother Denzil though, and those two were thick as thieves. They would meet up in the barn at night and wrestle until the early hours of the morn. And then one day in the middle of the night they got up and left, not even a note nor nothin. They never came back. Me dad was distraught, not only did he lose his finest farmhand John, but he lost his only son.

We found out a few years later they opened up a hairdressers in Pontypridd called 'British Hairways' and on the weekends would go to local nightclubs and sip cocktails in pink suits. I shed a tear or two when the divorce papers came through but it nearly killed me dad. He's barely got out of bed since, not even to go to the toilet like.

We went at it like two hungry Tamworth pigs

When John left I was determined to find meself a strappin fella. As me dad said, I was starting to 'over ripe' and I needed to be fertilised by a young bee before I rotted off the fruit tree. There was a gang of young lads in the village that would cycle up to the farm at night and peep through the window at me and me sisters when we were puttin our rollers in. Me dad used to chase em down the track with a cattle prod but that didn't put em off. One day they all came to the door dressed in suits and asked me dad if they could take me and me sisters to the fair. Me dad agreed on the condition that there would be no funny business unless they were willin

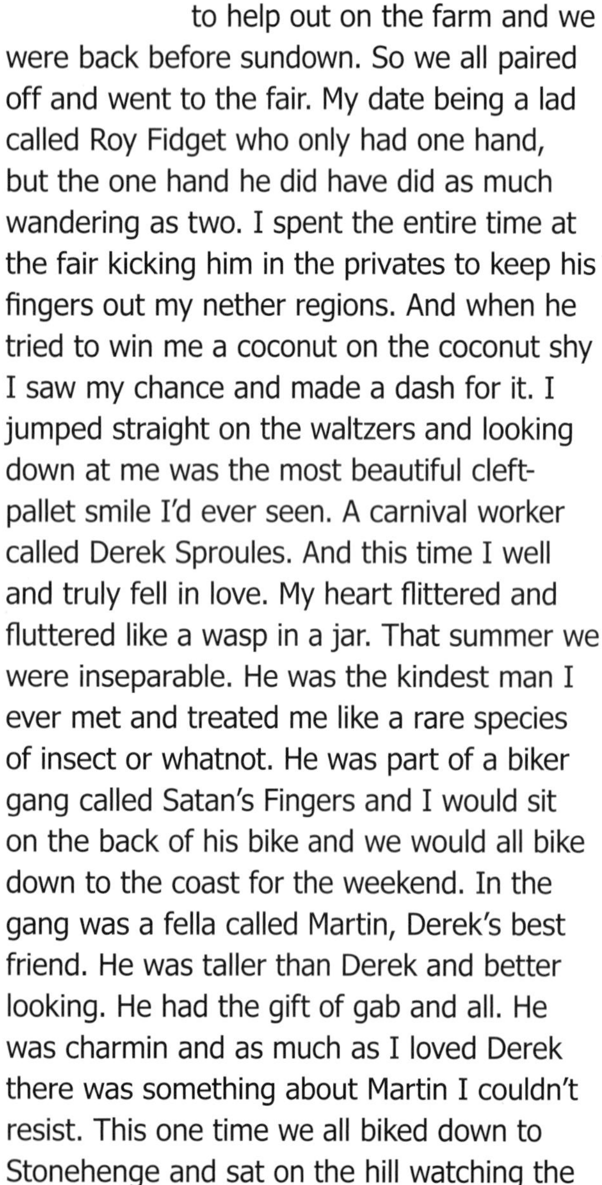

to help out on the farm and we were back before sundown. So we all paired off and went to the fair. My date being a lad called Roy Fidget who only had one hand, but the one hand he did have did as much wandering as two. I spent the entire time at the fair kicking him in the privates to keep his fingers out my nether regions. And when he tried to win me a coconut on the coconut shy I saw my chance and made a dash for it. I jumped straight on the waltzers and looking down at me was the most beautiful cleft-pallet smile I'd ever seen. A carnival worker called Derek Sproules. And this time I well and truly fell in love. My heart flittered and fluttered like a wasp in a jar. That summer we were inseparable. He was the kindest man I ever met and treated me like a rare species of insect or whatnot. He was part of a biker gang called Satan's Fingers and I would sit on the back of his bike and we would all bike down to the coast for the weekend. In the gang was a fella called Martin, Derek's best friend. He was taller than Derek and better looking. He had the gift of gab and all. He was charmin and as much as I loved Derek there was something about Martin I couldn't resist. This one time we all biked down to Stonehenge and sat on the hill watching the sun go down. Every time Derek nodded off, Martin was in me ear, flirtin with me rotten. There was somethin passionate about Martin and as sweet as Derek was, Martin was pure sex in a pair of cowboy boots. Later that evening I volunteered to go on a scrumpy run and Martin came with me. We went off and Martin pulled me in behind one of the stones and I'm ashamed to say I did the dirty on Derek with Martin. We went at it like two hungry Tamworth pigs. The best sex I ever had, but the worst decision I ever made. And when Derek came to investigate where we were, he saw it all, from start to finish. We were enjoyin it so much we didn't even realise Derek was stood there watching, tears rolling down his acne-scarred cheeks. That turned out to be the last time I saw Derek. That night he walked off and he just kept walking, all the way to Weston-super-Mare and into the sea. His body was never recovered expect for a single motorcycle boot washed up on Penarth Beach and a ring box with an engagement ring in it. Would I have said yes? Of course I would have, but in my heart of hearts I hadn't had me fill of Martin just yet.

His body was never recovered expect for a single motorcycle boot washed up on Penarth Beach

I never really had the chance to grieve for Derek cos Martin had me running round after him like a little lap dog. Three months later he proposed to me on my birthday with a nut bolt that he expanded in a vice after forgetting to buy me a present. We were married six months later in a registry office in Gloucester. The very same day a young couple were sat in the waiting room with us. 'Nervous?' said Martin. 'Nah', the man replied, 'Done it before.' It turned out to be Fred and Rose West. We ended up becoming good friends and would often go round theirs for a Sunday roast. Fred would always put too much cornflour in the gravy and never stir it in properly. You'd be eating your roast and suddenly have a mouth full of flour in yer gob.

I gave him the news that he was gonna be a father and he left so quickly he didn't even bother putting his boots on. He just walked out in the street in his socks.

I knew things were on the rocks with me and Martin when we would go to the pictures and he'd sit behind me and throw popcorn at me head. He would always take the mickey out me perm when we were among friends, saying things like, 'worst mistake I ever made, marrying a fat Kevin Keegan.' But things really came to a head when one Valentine's Day I said I was pregnant. I gave him the news that he was gonna be a father and he left so quickly he didn't even bother putting his boots on. He just walked out in the street in his socks. Months past and I found meself at the hospital on me own with a crying little bundle of misery called Kerry. She weighed 11lbs 7oz and was the spitting image of Rick Wakeman.

For a year I brought Kerry up as a single mum until I met Merlin, a wheelchair-bound metalhead who was a guitarist in a band called Fecal Matter. They were my favourite local band at the time and when they were playing at the Wheatsheaf down the road, I Sellotaped a bottle of milk to Kerry's crib, slid into me black leather trousers and strutted all the way down there in me stilettos like Olivia Newton John. There was somethin bout Merlin that set him apart from the rest. Not the fact he was in a wheelchair, but that he could do wheelies in his wheelchair while shredding his guitar. Like Derek did with his bike, I would sit on Merlin's lap and he'd wheel me home. After a few weeks he moved in and we'd spend countless evenings together, snuggled up watchin 'London's Burning' while Kerry was upstairs teaching herself how to walk and talk. She was always good like that Kerry, you'd just leave her alone in a room and she'd get on with it. We were a good family unit. Merlin would write songs in the shed while I cooked and did the housework. It was a happy home life for a good few months, until I discovered Merlin had a dark side. He was spending increasingly more amount of time in the shed 'writing songs' as he would put it, but I soon learnt he wasn't writing songs at all.

He had a dark secret, he was a pyromaniac, that's why he loved 'London's Burning' so much.

He had a dark secret, he was a pyromaniac, that's why he loved 'London's Burning' so much. He was using the shed to set fire to things. His favourite thing was to burn photographs cos it would burn colours you wouldn't be able to get from anywhere else. He was always obsessed with burnt things, like I'd put some sausages on the grill for a butty, and when I'd turn me back he would turn the grill up full volume and sniff in the burnt smell like it was Chanel No. 5. It should have dawned on me sooner, all the signs were there. The shed had caught on fire 12 times in the short 2 months of being with him. 'It's them darn mice doing it,' he'd say, 'kicking over the petrol can and setting it on fire with the friction of their bonking', and like a damn fool I believed him. Merlin had always told me he was in a wheelchair after his legs was run over in an electric tram accident, but I didn't know the truth. Merlin was in a wheelchair because he used to set his legs on fire on a regular basis. It was a sort of fetish I suppose, he'd douse his legs in lighter fuel then 'accidentally' drop a lit candle on his lap (to cover himself for insurance purposes). He would do this every day, he just couldn't get enough of the smell of his burnt legs. I peeked at em under the covers once, when we was getting down to it, he would always wear jeans, even in bed, but he'd taken them off this one and only time to help with his love making, and that's when I saw em. It was shockin – they were like two burnt twigs, no thicker than a pencil, and his feet just weren't there. Then I twigged as to why he always Sellotaped his jeans to his boots – cos he had no feet.

Then I twigged as to why he always Sellotaped his jeans to his boots – cos he had no feet.

I turned a blind eye to it, but what used to fill me with dread was every year when the 5th November came round, Bonfire Night, and I knew he could get his hands on as many standard fireworks as could satisfy his dark habit. Bonfire Night 1997, Merlin went missing, but I knew exactly where he was. I ran down to the park where a giant 'Guy Fawkes' effigy made from straw was about to be burned on a stake. I looked everywhere for him but Merlin was nowhere to be seen until suddenly I heard blood-curdlin screams coming from the flames of the burning effigy. It was Merlin, blisterin and cracklin like a hog on a spit. When no one was looking he had swapped clothes with the Guy Fawkes and pulled himself up on the stake with his arms ready to be burnt alive – his ultimate fantasy. His charred remains were found clutching a fire extinguisher, obviously in the hope he could enjoy it for a few minutes before he could put imself out. But unfortunately the flames were more than what he anticipated and he couldn't put himself out in time. We cremated him at St Mary's church cos I knew that's what he would have wanted and I went back to being a single mum.

A few years passed without much to note. Kerry was doing my head in as usual. She was just like a big hungry baby bird, always wanting bloody food, like a black hole of fish fingers and potato smilies. Her never ending appetite was beginnin to eat into Merlin's £500 inheritance and I soon realised it was time to get a job. But after a few months of trying, no one wanted to employ Kerry. 'She's too young,' they'd say, too young?! At 8 years old I was out on the farm slaughtering pigs with a bolt gun!! I don't say I regret having Kerry but if I had my chance to go back again I'd definitely make Martin wear a sheaf or at least finish himself off in a flannel.

One day there was a knock on the door. It was Martin wearin nothin but a thong and carryin a dartboard.

One day there was a knock on the door. It was Martin wearin nothin but a thong and carryin a dartboard. 'I made a mistake, I love you Sue, I always loved me women big,' he said. 'Who kicked you out this time?' I replied. 'Carol,' he said, 'She's a psycho and she's cut up all me clothes.' I looked at him for a minute, his great big puppy-dog eyes looking back at me. 'C'mon Sue, it's bloody freezin out here!' he said. 'Well...' I said, 'There's a shelf needs puttin up, the bathroom needs retiling and you can plaster in the hole you punched in the kitchen wall before you left.' He said, 'Fine, but you cook all me meals and never leave me alone with the kid.' I said 'fine' and he said 'fine'. So Martin moved back in for a bit. That was always like Martin, coming back with his cock between his legs when his other women had booted him out for doin the dirty of em. And anyway, after Merlin I was just grateful to be with anyone who didn't want to set themself on fire. That evening we snuggled up in front of the TV and watched 'Noel Edmond's House Party' and we were like the perfect family. Us laughin our heads off at Noel Edmunds and Kerry laughing her head off at Mr Blobby. Martin turned to me, looked me right in the eyes and said, 'Shall we give this a go Sue? For real this time?' I said 'yeah'. Next morning he was gone – shacked up with Jackie who worked at the Wimpy. And it wasn't long before she kicked him out after getting with Sally at the Social Club. Then Sally kicked him out and he was back with Carol.

you gotta make compromises to make relationships work. It's all about meetin in the middle. So after I watched him eating his ham omelette at Little Chef we drove to the Toby where he watched me have me breakfast.

A few more years trundled along. Kerry was startin secondary school. She was a lot bigger than the other kids, purely cos she was kept behind 5 years as her brain was a little slow

to get goin at times. Her brain was like a speedboat motor with water in it. You had to pull the string a few times to get it goin like. I was movin into middle age and was starting to feel lonesome without a fella round the house. But one day I picked up a CB radio from a car boot sale and ended up chatting to some truckers on it who were driving all up and down the country. I got particularly close to one trucker called Dallas and we'd spend hours chatting on his long-haul journeys to Brittany. After 6 months chatting to each other every night we ended up knowing everything about one and other. Then one night he said, 'Ere Sue, I'm delivering some U-bends next week to somewhere 20 minutes down the road from you, you fancy meeting up?' I agreed and the date was set. I was gonna meet Dallas at the Little Chef carpark just off the A419. I remember sitting there nervous as hell when suddenly I heard a knock on the car window and all I saw was a long big beard and a pair of kind eyes. 'Can I buy you a ham omelette breakfast from the Little Chef?' said Dallas. 'Well...' I said. 'There's a Toby Carvery up the road and they do an all you can eat breakfast, you can have as much bacon, sausages, eggs, baked beans, button mushrooms, toast and condiments as you want and there's even breakfast Yorkshire puddings and gravy and a cheese and potato bacon onion hash if you fancy that as well.' 'How much is it?' he said. '£3.99' I said. 'Can you go up as many times as you like?' he said. 'Within reason, you don't wanna take the piss like,' I said. 'Do you get a cup of tea included in that?' he said. 'No,' I said, 'but for 99p you can get a bottomless mug and have as much tea as you can drink' I said. 'How can they make any profit?' he said. 'Cos it's low quality ingredients,' I said. 'Thought as much,' he said. 'But little word of advice,' I said. 'Dont fill up your plate on your first go cos there will be breakfast items you end up likin more than others and the waitresses get a bit sniffy if you got loads left on your plate.' 'I suppose that's fair,' he said. 'So you fancy it?' I said. 'Nah, kind of got me heart set on the Little Chef ham omelette to be honest with yer,' he said. That's when I realised that sometimes you gotta make compromises to make relationships work. It's all about meetin in the middle. So after I watched him eating his ham omelette at Little Chef we drove to the Toby where he watched me have me breakfast. 'Bloody hell, you're like a bloody yo-yo,' he said. 'What dya mean?' I said. 'Up down up down to that breakfast buffet,' he said. 'Waste not want not,' I said. 'Ere, wrap that sausage in this serviette for laters will ya? and put some of them ketchups in your handbag an all,' he said. That's what I liked about Dallas, tight as a gnat's asshole. He used to make me dry out me teabags on the washing line after I used them. 40 cups of tea he could get out of one bag.

He could only ever sleep sitting up and holding something circular like a steering wheel

After breakfast he let me sit up front with him on his truck and we drove to the Esso garage where he showed me how he could wash himself in a public toilet with nothing but a paper towel and hand soap. He lived in his truck you see. 'Junction 6 off the M4 is my home sweet home,' he'd often say. That's what excited me about Dallas, he was a free spirit and didn't care who knew. 'Council tax?' he'd say, 'nah road tax more like', whatever that was supposed to mean, but I sort of got what he was saying, in a way.

For the next few months me and Dallas saw each other as much as we could in between his long-haul trucking jobs all over Europe. He was a kind man with a good moral compass. The only thing he wouldn't abide by was animal cruelty and Eddie Stobart drivers. 'Overpaid show offs,' he'd grunt whenever we would pass one on the motorway. 'They wouldn't know the first thing bout real trucking, and all the little kiddies waving at em like they're bloody pop stars,' he said.

'I'd like to see em on a long-haul truck job to Bratislava with no toilet stops and nothing but a bottle of Lucozade and a packet of chicken tikka Fridge Raiders to keep em going.' I liked how passionate Dallas was about truckin but whenever he stayed at mine he couldn't shake off some of his old habits. He could only ever sleep sitting up and holding something circular like a steering wheel, so I used to give him a plate to hold and put him to sleep on a kitchen chair. He used to be dreadful embarrassed about it but I found it was quite cute.

One night he picked me up in his truck and he drove me to a quiet little layby overlookin the Blunsdon bypass. We parked up and he switched the engine off. It was the most stunning view I'd ever seen. The orange from the traffic cones sparkled under the street lamps like fairies in orange dresses. The cat's eyes on the road dazzled like diamonds, and the roadwork signs reflected the odd car lamp like a roadwork sign reflecting a car lamp. Dallas turned to me and looked deep into my soul. 'I wanna settle down,' he said. My heart skipped a beat. 'I want a proper relationship like.' He popped the question and me and Dallas got engaged with a plan to be married by the autumn. I was the third happiest I'd ever been.

The wedding couldn't seem to come fast enough for Dallas. 'Let's just go down the registry office now and get on with it! What's with all the waiting like?!' But after my last two marriages I wanted to take me time and do it proper but Dallas simply couldn't understand it. We'd argue about it and he'd storm out and sit in his truck and rev his engine in anger. But I stood me ground and that was that. One day I came home from the bingo and Dallas shoved a piece of paper and pen in me hand and said, 'Will you sign this for me, love?' 'What is it?' I said. 'Oh it's nothing,' he said, 'just a consent form for Kerry's school trip to Wookey Hole.' 'Well when she goin?' I said. 'Does it matter??' he said. 'Well can I at least read the form before I sign it?' I said. 'Who reads forms before they bloody sign em?!!' he said. 'Well why has it got life insurance policy written on the top of it?' I said. 'Oh, you know them things, just in case Kerry gets hit by a big rock when she's down in one of the caves or whatnot,' he said. 'Chance will be a fine thing,' I said. 'Well can you just pass me my glasses so I can read it,' I said. 'God woman you're making such a big fuss over nothin!!' he said and stormed out. Dallas was getting in such a rage I just signed the bloody thing.

One day we went to see the registrar and they asked about our previous marriages. 'Just the twice for me, third time lucky this time!' I said laughing. '9th time for me,' said Dallas being all coy and that. 'You been divorced 8 times?!' I said shocked. 'No, widowed, they all fell down the stairs and died unfortunately.' He said. 'Oh that's terrible luck,' I said. 'Yeah bless em,' he said.

He was bouncing off the walls like Flubber in the film 'Flubber'

Our wedding day arrived and I've never seen Dallas so excited. He was bouncing off the walls like Flubber in the film 'Flubber'. The day went without a hitch and we became husband and wife. At our reception we had huge bowls of cheesy chips. You can't go wrong with cheesy chips. Then evening came and we were off on our honeymoon to Weston-super-Mare like two excited little kiddies. We checked into the B&B where Dallas handed me a glass of fizz. 'Tastes a bit bitter,' I said to Dallas. 'What you mean?' he said. 'It tastes like crushed up Nytol,' I said. 'Oh stop your moaning and get it down your neck,' he said. I refused to drink it and poured it down the sink. That's when Dallas put his hands round me throat. 'What are you doin?!' I said. 'Giving you a throat massage,' he said. 'But I can't breathe,' I said. 'Yeah that's how they do it in Thailand,' he said. 'But I'm passin out,' I said. 'Yeah that's how they do it in Thailand,' he said.

Next thing I know, I wake up in a hospital bed with a lovely lookin policeman fella looking over me. 'You're a very lucky woman,' he said. 'Where's Dallas?' I asked. 'Dallas? You mean Dave Miller the Trucker Killer?' And blow me, Dallas was trying to kill me this whole time and I never suspected a thing. But it's just like what the late and great Freddie Mercury once said, 'Too much love will kill yer', and it almost did, if it weren't for the thickness of me neck that cushioned me windpipe when he was stranglin me. The police had arrested Dallas at customs in Dover and in the back of his truck found a rope, balaclava, a shovel and enough acid to erode an entire fully grown hippopotamus. Dallas had thought I was dead and was planning on taking out my life insurance to start a new life in Zakynthos where he dreamed of opening an American-themed bar on the beach called Dave's Place. Well like I said to the nice young police officer, the only bar he's gonna be servin behind is the ones in Her Majesty's prison. And he laughed and laughed. 'You don't fancy goin on a date do yer officer?' I said. 'Nah you're alright,' he said. 'Fair enough,' I said. And that was that.

I decided to knock courtin on the head all together after Dallas. I've seen Martin a few times but that was only to satisfy our own needs. To be honest I'm quite happy on me own and anyway Kerry is still around to file me corns and that. Deep down I'll still be waiting for my prince charming to sweep me off my feet but unless Poldark or Hornblower are single I aint really bothered. End of.

MARTIN MUCKLOWE'S BUILDING SITE RULES

Martin Mucklowe Contractors

NO JOB
TOO SMALL

EST. 1994

Best in the West (since Fred West)

BUILDING SITE RULES

Martin Mucklowe Contractors rules state:

- **NO** moaning.
- **NO** complaining.
- **NO** negative Nancys.
- **NO** clowning around. If you don't like the work, the circus is in town and they are always looking for clowns.
- Cake Tuesday. Every Tuesday is Cake Tuesday, where you bring in a cake that you have baked yourself for everyone to share. Whoever bakes the least tasty cake must get the rounds in at the Keepers.
- Jokes. Martin is the only person to makes jokes on site. If you think you have a good joke to tell, clear it through Dan first.
- **NO** negative talk about Swindon Town.

- **NO** negative talk about Luke Norris.
- Lunch is 30 minutes, any longer and it gets taken out your wage packet.
- **NO** high-viz jackets. We ain't lollipop ladies!
- Any dirty mug left in the van, apart from Martin's, will be smashed on the road by Dan.
- **NO** salad for lunch! Only white bread doorstop sandwiches allowed, with either ham or cheese filling.
- **NO** vaping, only smoking on site.
- Only music allowed on the sound system is Status Quo, with the exception of Humble Pie, on occasion. Must be played at full volume.
- **NO** first aid kits allowed. Any injuries should be treated with cold water. A shot of whisky may be administered for pain control. Two shots if your arm or leg is hanging off.
- Tea must be strictly builder's tea. Anyone caught drinking Earl Grey or Lapsang will be booted off site forthwith.
- Nudes. If you receive any nudes from your missus whilst on site these must be shared immediately. Martin has first dibs on these pictures should he need a Portaloo wank.

Vintage Steam Fair

Saturday 24th and Sunday 25th June
at Pengford Green, 11am–4 pm.

Featuring working traction engines,
road rollers and vintage steamers.

Events include the world famous Vintage
Steamer Parade and the popular combine
demonstration hosted by 'four times
English combine champion' **Jim Tucker.**

And back by popular demand –
'The Dorset Dancing Diggers' (see photo).

Other attractions include: car boot and trade
stands, arm wrestling competition and mashed
potato eating contest.

Admission fee £5

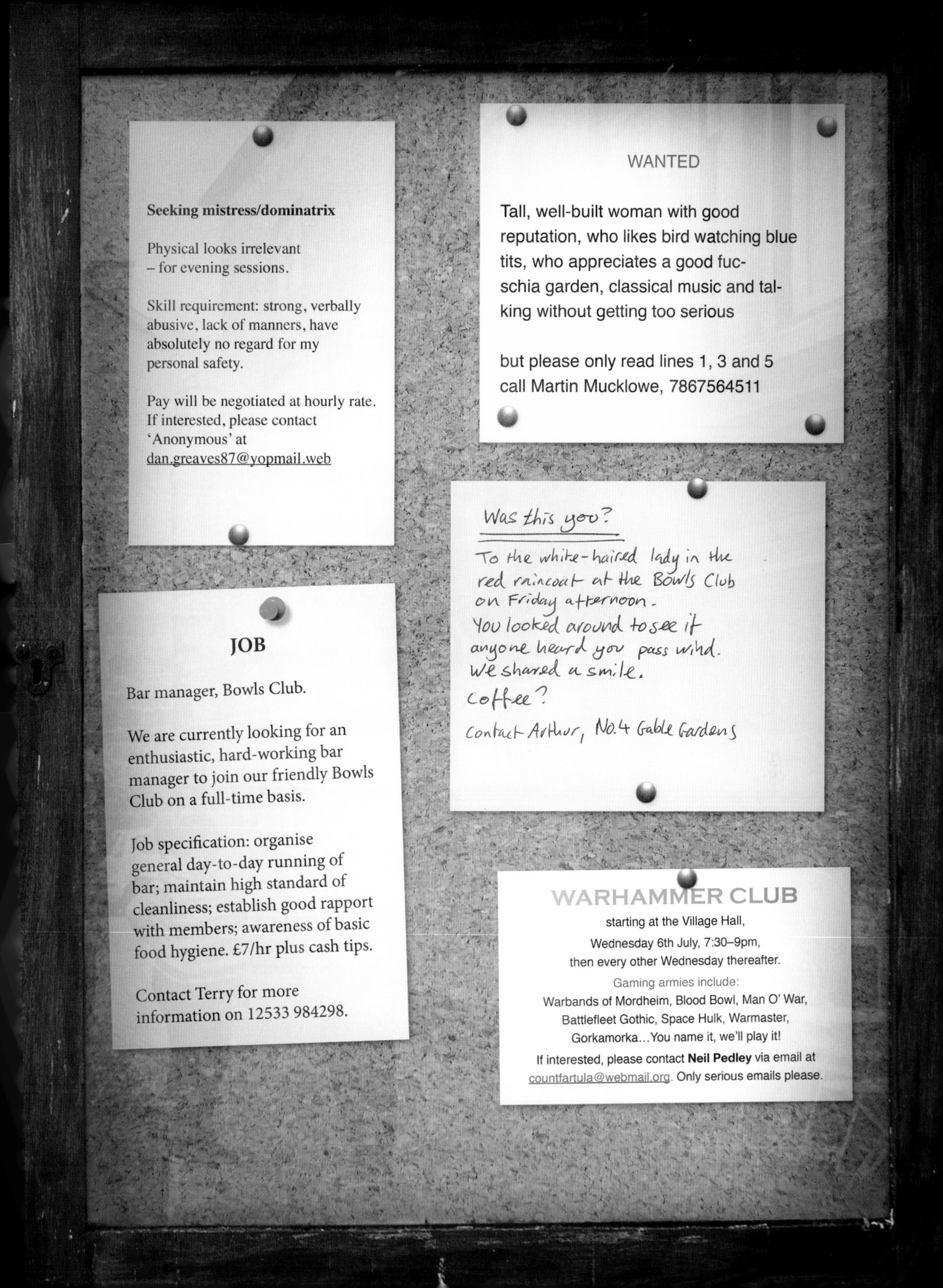

Seeking mistress/dominatrix

Physical looks irrelevant
– for evening sessions.

Skill requirement: strong, verbally abusive, lack of manners, have absolutely no regard for my personal safety.

Pay will be negotiated at hourly rate. If interested, please contact 'Anonymous' at dan.greaves87@yopmail.web

WANTED

Tall, well-built woman with good reputation, who likes bird watching blue tits, who appreciates a good fuc-
schia garden, classical music and tal-
king without getting too serious

but please only read lines 1, 3 and 5
call Martin Mucklowe, 7867564511

Was this you?

To the white-haired lady in the red raincoat at the Bowls Club on Friday afternoon.
You looked around to see if anyone heard you pass wind.
We shared a smile.
Coffee?
Contact Arthur, No.4 Gable Gardens

JOB

Bar manager, Bowls Club.

We are currently looking for an enthusiastic, hard-working bar manager to join our friendly Bowls Club on a full-time basis.

Job specification: organise general day-to-day running of bar; maintain high standard of cleanliness; establish good rapport with members; awareness of basic food hygiene. £7/hr plus cash tips.

Contact Terry for more information on 12533 984298.

WARHAMMER CLUB

starting at the Village Hall,
Wednesday 6th July, 7:30–9pm,
then every other Wednesday thereafter.

Gaming armies include:
Warbands of Mordheim, Blood Bowl, Man O' War, Battlefleet Gothic, Space Hulk, Warmaster, Gorkamorka…You name it, we'll play it!

If interested, please contact **Neil Pedley** via email at countfartula@webmail.org. Only serious emails please.

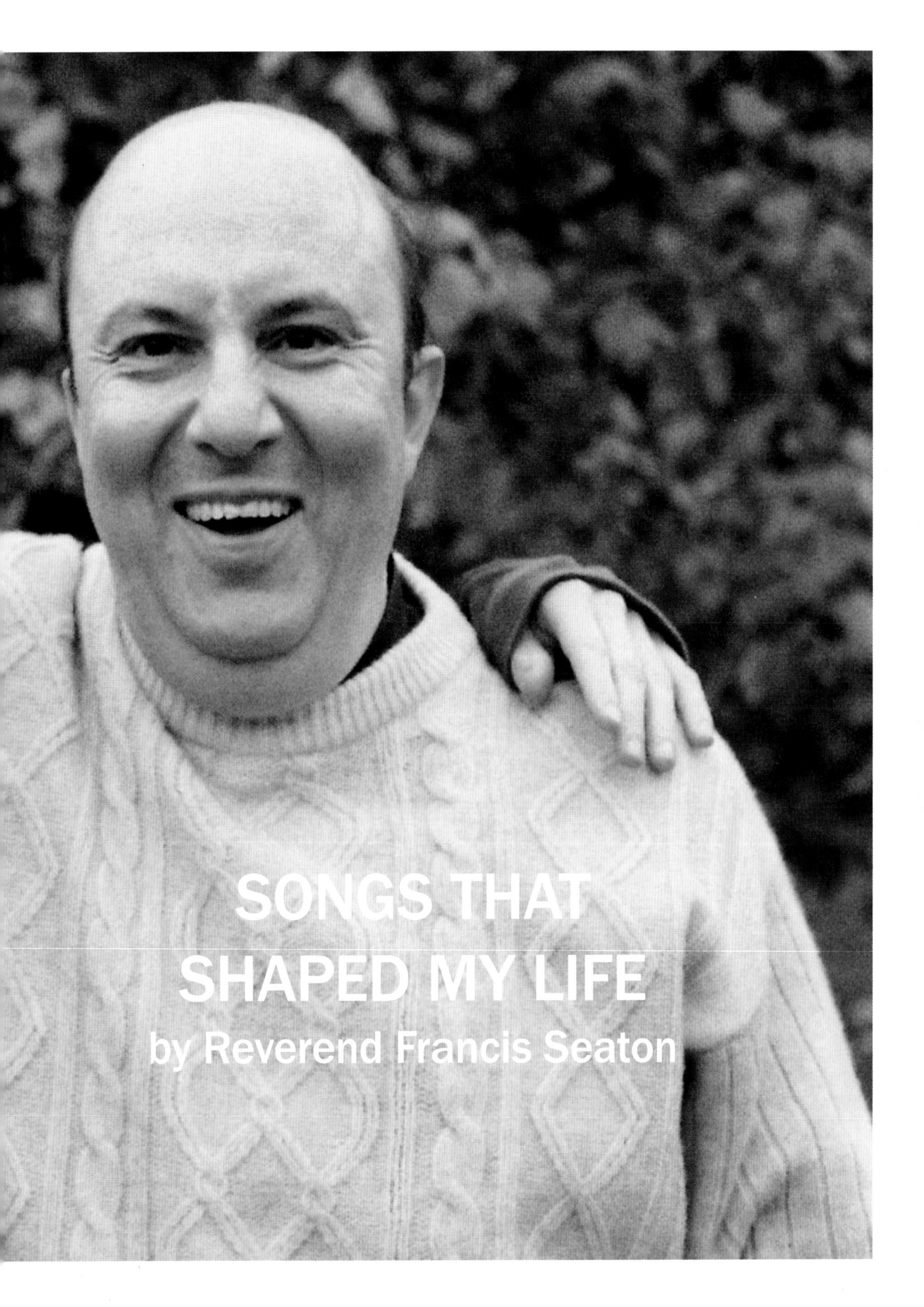
SONGS THAT
SHAPED MY LIFE
by Reverend Francis Seaton

Songs That Shaped My Life

'Baker Street'

Gerry Rafferty

The first record I bought when I was about 8 years old, way back in the late 70s. I was totally nutty about this song, particularly the sax solo, and would play it over and over and over – much to my parents' dismay. I was so obsessed with the song I even made a paper saxophone, which I played so much I ended up inhaling it and spending two nights in a children's hospital having it removed. I'll never forget looking at an X-ray of my lungs and seeing a paper saxophone entangled in my bronchioles. I remember the nurse saying to me, 'If you don't become a musician, this will all have been a waste of time.'

Stand And Deliver

Adam and the Ants

My first memory of truly belonging to a 'music scene' was when I first saw Adam and the Ants at the Exeter Corn Exchange in 1981, and WOW what a group. The whole 'New Romantic' movement was everything I had been waiting for, and, as a young teenager growing up in sleepy north Devon, it was pure fantastical escapism. The hair, the fashion, the music and, above all, the gentlemanly attitude. I felt it coursing through my veins. Growing up in the country meant that trends took a little longer to catch on, and we discovered we were often months or even years behind the latest hairstyles and fashions seeping out of London. That all changed, however, when my auntie brought me back the latest copy of the *NME* from London. On the front cover was Adam Ant, sporting a wickedly cool tricornered hat. I immediately gathered up my pocket money and rushed down to my nearest antique shop and purchased an 18th-century Napoleonic hat, which didn't move from my head for the next 12 months. I was the talk of Colehurst Comprehensive for the whole of that morning. I remember my father taking a particular dislike to my new purchase and he would often rib me in front of his friends. I remember, this one time, I got home from school and he pulled me into the smoking room, 'Look at my son, Francis!' he said, 'Look how wide his silly hat is! We'll have to take the doorframes out so he can fit through the doors!' His friends laughed and laughed and laughed but I didn't care, and replied, 'I'm the dandy highwayman who you're too scared to mention, I spend my cash on looking flash and grabbing your attention.' But when I swung round to punctuate my statement, my hat accidentally knocked off and smashed one of my mother's favourite picture frames. It hurt my mother tremendously. Fashion is all well and good, but as soon as it starts hurting the people you love, you know it's time to stop.

West End Girls

Pet Shop Boys

When this synth-pop duo burst onto the scene in the mid 80s, my life took a rather interesting detour. The music was like nothing I had ever heard, and, as an angst ridden teenager with dermatology problems, this group really provided an identity for me – a belonging, if you will. You weren't just a fan of the Pet Shop Boys. It was a way of life. They inspired me to trundle off down to my local music store and purchase my first synthesiser with money I saved up from working as an usher at the pictures. The summer of 1985, I locked myself away in my bedroom and taught myself the instrument. It was the beginning of a long love affair with synth pop. Later that summer, I formed a band with some chaps from my 6th Form maths class called Go Eat 3.14, which was a playful pun on our favourite equation and our favourite food, but no one seemed to get it, so after a few shows we changed our name to The Equations. We may not have been the most musically gifted, but we were certainly avant-garde, and pricked up a few ears at our Student's Union with a string of fairly raucous shows. But the band split after a fairly scathing review in our student paper by some snotty little first year, who wrote of the band, 'I've come to the conclusion that The Equations = 0 talent + 0 musical direction x pomposity of the highest level. And how old is the synth player because he's balding on top, he could do with adding some more prime numbers to his hairline. If I was a teacher marking this equation, I'd write in red "Please see me".' I often think back to that review and how unnecessarily vile it was. I stand by the belief that if you don't have anything nice to say, don't say anything at all. The reviewer turned out to have a rather successful career as a disc jockey and television presenter. His name was Mark Lamarr.

Despite the knockback, I wasn't quite done with music yet, and, whilst at university studying theology, I formed a new band with a couple of fellow trainee vicars. We had intended to call ourselves The Dog Collars, but as Peter pointed out, it could have been considered crass and a tad blasphemous to the man upstairs, so we settled on the name The Nice Guys, as we thought this was as inoffensive as you can get. So many bands at the time were trying to be like the Sex Pistols, smashing up their instruments and saying rude

Songs That Shaped My Life *continued*

things about the Queen, but we didn't find that cool. We looked after our instruments and made sure that we polished them with a yellow duster and layer of Mr Sheen before they went back into their monogrammed cases. That was our cool, that was our image. We were the sort of guys you'd find at a house party going round with a binbag picking up the empties.

The group had a different feel to the band before as we were all talented musicians in our own right. We had Peter Probert, a whizz on the electronic harp, and John Tibbet, a classically trained guitarist who made the great Andrés Segovia sound like he was playing a loose fishing line over an empty Kleenex box. I, of course, was on the synth, as well as lead singer, which suited me well as my late pubescence meant I could still reach the falsetto notes others of the same age could not. We spent months writing and rehearsing, and were finally ready to take our music out into the world. We had what we thought was a hit single in the song 'Good Guy' and couldn't wait for the people to hear it, so we organised our very first headline tour, starting at Barnstaple YMCA, north Devon, and ending at Lynton Model Railway Village. It was 1988, and the tour turned out to be a financial disaster; playing to half empty rooms and village halls wasn't really what we had expected. We also had our fair share of shady band managers, one of whom duped us out of £7,000 (a lot of money in those days) and left us stranded by the side of the motorway after a gig in Stranraer (but that's another story!). In desperation, we decided to put all our last pennies together and buy coach tickets to London, armed with demo tapes in the

by Reverend Francis Seaton

hope we could secure a record deal once and for all. Without much of a plan we decided to head straight to Virgin Records on Oxford Street, but once we got there we didn't really know what to do, so just hung around outside the shop in the hope that perhaps a music industry mogul would find our look kooky and sign us to their record label. It wasn't quite as simple as that, and all we came across was a barrage of angry shoppers. To make things worse, on our way back to the tube station we got lost in Soho, which was an extremely dangerous place for three young trainee vicars back in the late 80s, and we ended up missing our coach back to north Devon. Not knowing what to do and with panic beginning to set in, we flagged down a patrolling policeman and told him our situation. He just laughed and said, 'What do you expect me to do about it?' Peter began to cry, while I silently prayed for God to send us help. Suddenly, a tall Dutch man ear-wigging our conversation offered us a place to stay for the night. He said he only lived a couple of streets away. I thanked the Lord and we followed him to his accommodation. His name was Bert Jan, he remained silent for most of the walk but told us about his flatmate Berk, and the crazy midnight feasts Berk and him would have. The walk to his flat seemed to get longer and longer. It had definitely been a couple of hours of stomping and we had most certainly ventured outside of Central London. Bert Jan's pupils seemed to be extremely large, I could barely see the whites of his eyes. I was starting to get the heebie-jeebies about Bert Jan, but Peter seemed so relaxed that he started holding hands with Bert Jan whilst they played 'I spy' as we were walking. When we finally got there, it was a rather grim-looking tower block. The lift apparently wasn't working as a fellow had been stabbed in it the night before and it was locked off, waiting for a dust around from forensics.

When we finally reached the apartment on the 11th floor, we found Bert Jan's flatmate, Berk, dancing around in a tank top and a sarong in the dark to a record he was playing backwards. The floor was littered with teaspoons and tin foil, which I suspected had something to do with the 'crazy midnight feasts' that Bert Jan had told us about. Bert Jan kindly offered us a seat on a makeshift sofa, which was made from a stack of building bricks with a few bloodstained cushions on top, while he went off into a bedroom with Peter to show him his records. John and I sat uncomfortably on the sofa as Berk continued to dance. He started looking in the mirror and talking about how much he wanted to be on the other side of it. Suddenly, Berk became aggressive, 'What the f*** you doing here, Grandad?!' he said, jabbing an eyeliner pencil at me. John gripped my hand tightly; being a year younger than Peter and I, he was the baby of the group and I knew I had to protect him. Bert started yelling in Dutch and heading over in our direction. Thinking on my feet, I grabbed John's hand and we rushed into the bathroom and locked the door. The crazed Bert

Songs That Shaped My Life *continued*

was banging on the door outside, trying to get in. We were trapped. John was crying uncontrollably. I looked up and saw an air vent just big enough to fit our slim, naive frames into. I pulled off the grate and we slithered through, coming out into the lobby of the tower block. We raced down those 11 flights of stairs faster than Linford Christie on jet-powered roller-skates. Our survival instinct had well and truly kicked in, and we left without Peter, who was still inside. We ran till our feet bled to Victoria Coach Station and caught the next coach home that morning. We only felt safe when the bus began to pull away.

The band split and we never saw Peter again, he dropped out of his theological studies and moved to London permanently. The last I heard he was a head teacher at an all-boys grammar school in Berkshire. John, however, completed his studies and graduated with the highest distinctions, but the following few decades were tough on him. He struggled with bouts of agoraphobia which left him living the life of a hermit crab in his mother's loft conversion – only venturing out for more doughnuts and a browse at the odd boot sale. A few years ago, his face popped up on television, being interviewed by Richard Madeley on 'This Morning' for having the largest BMI in England. I often think his troubles may have been triggered by the ordeal we shared together.

The experience put me off London for life. The only time I ever ventured back was to watch *The Lion King* with Polly on her birthday, but I could hardly enjoy it. I spent the entire time in the auditorium looking over my shoulder for Bert Jan. I don't know what Hell is, but I'm pretty sure it's a flat on the 11th floor in a tower block somewhere in London inhabited by two crazed Dutch men who like to listen to LPs backwards and wear eyeliner. Lord knows what became of Berk and Bert Jan, but one can only pray for their troubled souls.

The Boys Are Back In Town

Thin Lizzy

This song marks the next stage of my life, which was a fairly riotous few years. After university, I had my heart set on becoming a vicar and decided to carry out the necessary steps to do so. I enrolled in a vicar college in Somerset, where I would spend the next few years learning my trade. Every year, we were put on a coach

by Reverend Francis Seaton

to spend the summer at Buckfast Abbey to help out maintaining the abbey and grounds. It was an absolute riot, we were served the fortified wine at supper and once the Abbot had gone to bed, we would sneak out of our dorms, past the Abbot's quarters, shimmy down the drainpipes and wreak utter havoc. We would skinny-dip in the abbey pond, then climb over the ground walls to the nunnery, where we would hide in bushes and throw small pebbles at the nuns' windows to get them to come out. We were often chased back to the abbey by the Reverend Mother, who was hot on foot, equipped with a large whipping cane. Brother Adam was rather large and slow at getting over the nunnery wall, and in mid climb his bare bottom, lit by the full moon, was in perfect range and height for Reverend Mother's cane. All I'll say is the next morning at breakfast he was sat on three prayer cushions feeling very sorry for himself indeed.

Take On Me

A-ha

I played this song at my ordination. It was a moment of particular fulfilment of a journey that I had been on for many years. After eight years training to be a vicar, I was finally ready and willing for God to take me on, so what better song to play than 'Take On Me' by A-ha. When the ceremony finished, I'll never forget my brothers lifting me above their heads and carrying me out of the church as a fully-fledged vicar as I sang the chorus of the song at the top of my voice. We ate our packed lunch under the falling cherry blossom in the parish orchard and cracked open a bottle of homemade elderflower cordial to celebrate. I remember brother Tim accusing me of trumping, but I insisted it was

Songs That Shaped My Life *continued*

just the smell of my egg and cress sandwiches. For the record, I really didn't trump, but brother Tim didn't let it go, which did slightly tarnish the day.

Lady in Red

Chris de Burgh

This song has a particular significance for me as it reminds me of the first and only time I ever fell in love, with my dear wife, Polly. We met at a charity masquerade ball at Westonbirt Arboretum shortly after securing my first parish job in Tetbury. I was very close to not even going at all that night, but I remember brother Tim saying, 'Joseph didn't find his Mary by sitting in the rectory all day eating junk food and watching episodes of "Father Ted."' And he couldn't have been more right. I got up and got dressed, but didn't have a mask to wear; then suddenly remembered the mask I had given to me by the NHS when I broke my nose in a kayaking accident. It was a little bloodied, so I painted it black and attached a few curtain tassels on the ends, which really set me apart from the rest – especially when I was bopping about on the dancefloor and the tassels would go round in a circular motion like a propeller, so much so that I felt I could almost lift off the dancefloor. Looking back, I was very much peacocking, but didn't realise it at the time. From across the dancefloor, I remember seeing a meek girl with beautiful shoulder-length mousy hair and wearing a white dress that had shoulder pads so large it was as if she was smuggling two television sets on her shoulders. I immediately saw a kindred spirit, a wallflower desperate to stand out. 'Have you been to the arboretum before?' I asked. 'No, this is my first time,' she replied. 'Oh, you really must see those magnolia macrophylla while the leaves are still showing,' I said. 'I don't care much for trees,' she laughed. I think that's what drew me to Polly, her wicked sense of humour. Suddenly we were interrupted when a man pulled Polly by the arm and said, 'Come on fatso, let's get you home.' 'I beg your pardon?!' I said, feeling the two small glasses of Malbec starting to raise my testosterone levels. 'That's no way to talk to a lady,' I snapped. Without saying a word, the man pulled on my tassels and let go so the mask snapped back on my face. He laughed so much he was bent over double, slapping his knees and tears of laughter rolling down his cheeks. Suddenly the song 'Tiger Feet' by Mud started to play and I used it as a strategic device to stamp on his feet in time to the music. He immediately clocked on to my passive-aggressive dance moves and biffed me

by Reverend Francis Seaton

on the nose so hard I fell back into a giant bowl of cheese straws. 'Sorry about my brother,' said Polly. 'He has Intermittent Explosive Disorder, which is characterised by explosive outbursts of anger and violence, often to the point of rage that are disproportionate to the situation at hand.' 'Not to worry,' I replied, feeling rather mortified. That night, Polly drove me to the local A&E, blood streaming down my face and my nose so far across my cheek I looked like a Picasso painting (the NHS protective nose guard in this instance proving futile). We sat in the hospital waiting room and I looked at Polly under the bright strip lighting, her white dress now sodden with my red blood. Despite this, I couldn't stop thinking how beautiful she was and now every time I hear the song 'Lady in Red' by Chris de Burgh I think of her.

Why Does It Always Rain on Me?

Travis

This song reminds me of a particularly tough week I had in 1999. Our boiler stopped working, my son Jacob was in bed with chicken pox, and the Bishop had overheard me in the toilet criticising his sermon to my friend James while I was in the urinals and the Bishop was in the cubicle. Oh, how I died of embarrassment and shame when I clocked the tip of the Bishop's hat above the cubicle door. That evening I got into my Ford Focus and drove like a maniac along the backroads of the village, singing along to this song at full volume until my petrol light came on. This song struck a particular chord with me, as I did in fact lie when I was 17. Well, maybe not a lie, but I certainly over-exaggerated the success of my band The Equations to a fashion student called Sally who I was desperate to impress. I somehow believed that was the cause of all my troubles. It was the closest I had been to a midlife crisis, but thankfully Polly taking me bird-watching the next day at a local wetland centre saved me from tipping over the edge.

Father & Son

Cat Stevens

This song will always remind me of my son, Jacob. Having a son is a wonderful thing. As much as you want them to be mini versions of you, they will always be their own person, and so they should be. It hasn't always been an easy ride with Jacob, but he is very much a free spirit, and I have always respected that despite some of his life choices. Jacob was never a naughty boy at home but at school I was concerned with his friendship group, who I can only describe as

Songs That Shaped My Life *continued*

'rotten eggs' – and you know what they say about rotten eggs: if you place one in the carton, you're sure to spoil the others. When he was 15, I caught him smoking 'pot' in his room. I found myself at a crossroads. Do I discipline him or reach out to him? I did what I wish my father had done to me and communicated with him the best way I knew how: through music. I got my guitar, sat him down and played him the song 'Father and Son' by Cat Stevens. However, I underestimated quite how strong the cannabis fumes were in his airless room and upon reaching the second verse found myself utterly intoxicated, almost to the point of paralysis. Then a ravenous hunger came over me, which Jacob described as a bout of 'the munchies', and we subsequently bonded over rifling through the pantry cupboard until we came across a homemade coffee cake that Polly had baked for the Macmillan's coffee morning the next day. We devoured it whilst watching episodes of 'Family Guy' in the living room. I then woke up fully clothed in the spare bedroom, under a duvet covered in vomited coffee cake. When I tried to get up, I also discovered (and there's no nice way of saying this) that I had fouled the bed. Polly was so upset she drove all the way to West Sussex and spent the weekend with her parents. No amount of airing, scrubbing and Febreze could save the mattress, and unfortunately I ended up having to burn it on a bonfire in the back garden along with my chinos and Crew cardigan. Polly ended up replacing the mattress with an extremely extortionate one that she bought from John Lewis on credit. I'm still paying for that mattress today. Financially and emotionally!

by Reverend Francis Seaton

The Bishop

Les Misérables

The 2012 musical film *Les Misérables* is a favourite of mine. Every song moves me to the point of tears. I have always loved the story of Les Mis and I believe it has had a profound effect on my life, particularly the character of the Bishop of Digne, who I like to think I have modelled myself on since reading the novel years back. As a vicar, you come across many interesting people, just like the Bishop would have all those years ago. Some will test you, and it's your duty as a man of the Lord to show them nothing but love and compassion. When I first met Kerry and Kurtan, they were seeking sanctuary in the church from a furious Mr Wix after stealing an entire carton of Panini football stickers from the shop. I followed the trail of discarded sticker wrappers down the church pathway, through the church doors and to the 12th-century stained-glass windows, which were plastered in roughly 200–300 football stickers. Standing by the font were a very young Kerry and Kurtan, trying to push each other's heads into the water. Before I had time to do anything, Mr Wix burst through the door demanding that they come out immediately for him to walk them to the police station. I could easily have handed Kerry and Kurtan over to Mr Wix to be punished accordingly, but instead copied the actions of the Bishop in *Les Misérables* when he defended the captured Valjean after he steals silverware from the Bishop. The Bishop explains to the police that he gave the silverware to Valjean, despite the fact he hadn't, in the hope that Valjean would use this kind gesture to lead an honest life for as long as he lives. I told Mr Wix that I had asked Kerry and Kurtan to get me the stickers from the shop but forgot to give them the money. I pulled out my wallet. 'How much do I owe you?' I asked. '£400,' he replied. I almost fainted on the spot. 'Very well…' I said and handed him over the money. 'You must be very keen to finish your sticker album?' he said. I tried to speak but no words came out. When Mr Wix left, I walked up to Kerry and Kurtan, and with the precise words of the Bishop of Digne, said, 'Do not forget, never forget, that you have promised to use this money in becoming honest people.' Admittedly, they didn't know what I was talking about, but it felt appropriate at the time. A few years on and we're still working on them becoming a bit more honest, but like most things, it's a work in progress.

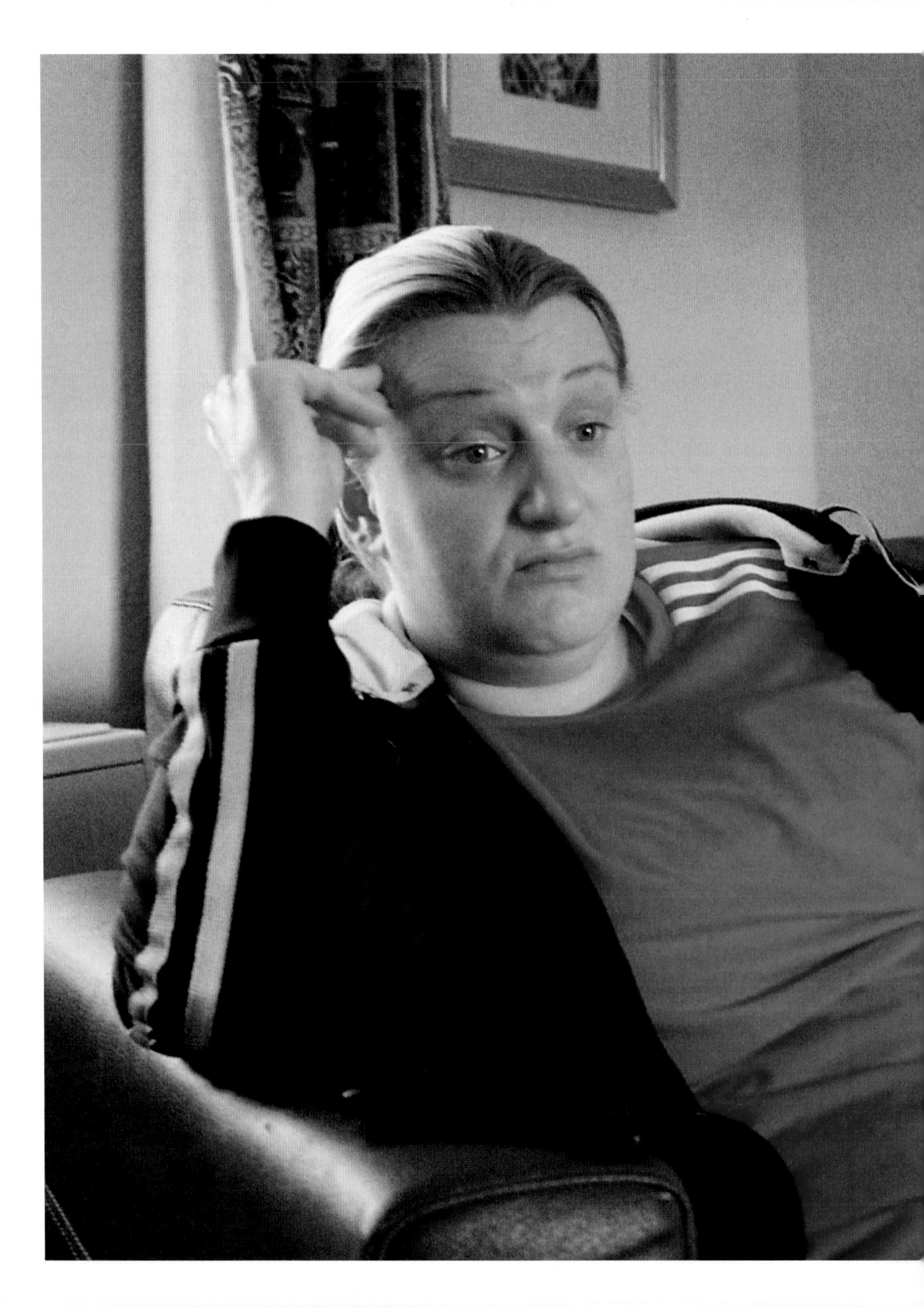

THINGS THAT USED TO EXIST THAT NO LONGER EXIST

by Kerry Mucklowe

Things That Used To Exist That No Longer Exist

Woolworths

Where I learnt all my shoplifting skills, mostly on the pick and mix. The day Woolworths closed was the day the world started falling apart. I'm not being funny but everything has just gone from bad to worse since. I blame the Woolworths curse.

Dial up internet

Sounded like an orchestra of clangers. It's mad to think we'll never hear the words 'get off the internet I need to use the phone' ever again.

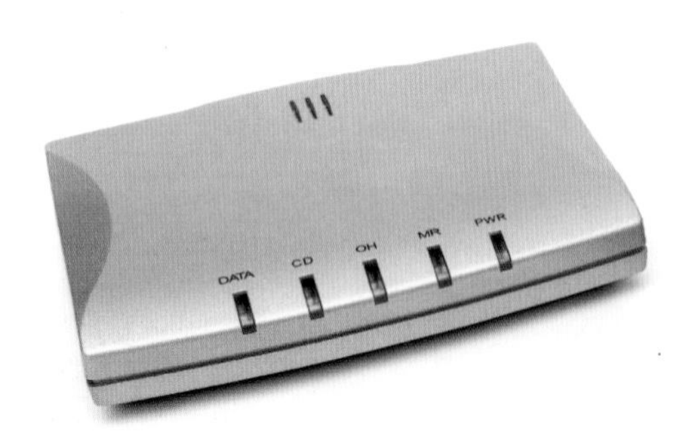

Beehive Bedlam

A game on Sky that you usually played to kill some time before the Simpsons came on at 6. Kurtan lost an entire summer playing this absolute brainwashing evil and almost got rickets because of it. His legs were so bowed he actually ended up looking like a bee. If I remember correctly his nan went through six Sky remotes which Kurtan smashed in frustration not being able to get past level 19.

Townies

Never hear about Townies anymore. In the late 90s/early 2000s they were everywhere but now, not a peep. Then the word 'Chav' came in and wiped Townies off the face of the earth.

Mini disc players

Absolute fad. Massive waste of time. Pure gimmick. Kurtan being a sucker for gimmicks got one for Christmas and would walk around the village listening to it like a dog with two dicks. But because the mini discs were so expensive he could only afford one album which was Macy Gray's 'On How Life Is' and there was only one good song on the album cos the rest was shite. Sweet justice in my humble opinion.

Strangers

There used to be loads around when I was a kid, especially in parks or hanging around school gates and that but now you never hear about them. They were always desperate to whisk you off with the promises of sweets and puppies. Shame they never really took off.

by Kerry Mucklowe

Donkeys at the seaside

These little beauties used to line the sands at Weston-super-Mare but these days you'll find them mostly seeking sponsorship in donkey sanctuaries. I don't mind paying a quid to ride one up and down the shoreline whilst its vertebrae buckles beneath my weight cos at least they're providing me with a service, but now they want money for absolutely nothing while they sit down and waft flies away from their shitty asses with their tails. These days their only use is for horse owners to keep them in a paddock to keep their horse company. What a pathetic life to live.

Things That Used to Exist *continued*

Game Boy printers

Back before selfies you could take a picture of yourself on a Game Boy and print it out but it was so pixelated you couldn't tell if it was a picture of you or a cat's arsehole.

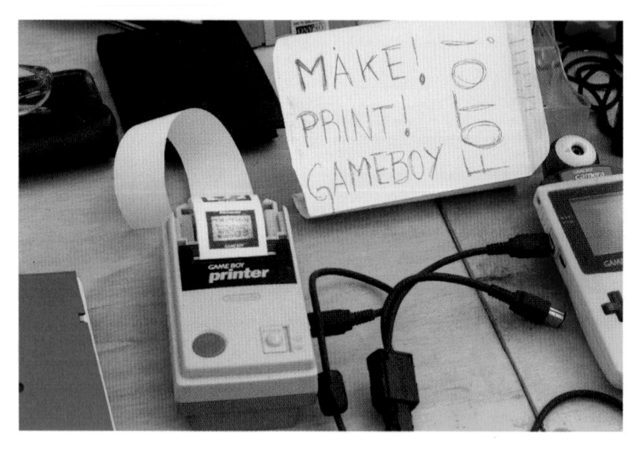

Turkey Twizzlers

Thanks to Jamie Oliver these no longer exist and I will never forgive him for that.

Demon Headmaster

I don't know where the Demon Headmaster starts and John Major ends. Have you ever seen them both in the same room? I think not.

The ozone layer

Whatever happened to the ozone layer? Did it actually disappear in the end cos that's all what Newsround and Blue Peter banged on about for years. I was made to feel like an absolute criminal for spraying on my Lynx Atlantis every morning and then everybody just forgot about it. These days it's all about plastic in the ocean and before the ozone layer it was all about sending foil milk bottle caps to Mozambique. How the fuck you supposed to build schools and hospitals with foil milk bottle caps?! Madness.

CD wallet cases

Used to find these in the bottom of car footwells with dusty boot prints on them. Most of the CDs inside consisted of those shitty free music CDs you'd get in Sunday newspapers. The Vicar collected them and had about a thousand of the damn things. Each and every one had the songs 'Would I Lie to You' and 'Moving On Up' on, perfect for the Vicar's crap music taste.

by Kerry Mucklowe

Mad Cow Disease

What happened to Mad Cow Disease? And how mad were these cows? Like 'evil genius' mad? Or 'Dorris from Pearly Crescent who collects conch shells and talks to the squirrels' mad? One of the most insulting things ever said to me was in Year 8 when I couldn't spell the word 'column' and Neville Parker said 'what's wrong with you, mad cow disease?' It was particularly upsetting to come from a boy who was constantly in therapy for having an infatuation with wiping his bottom on his mum's curtains.

Dub Step

It flew out as quick as it flew in and sounded like R2-D2 getting electrocuted by C-3PO's spunk when he blows his metal load in his face to a picture of a fuse box. Absolute nonsense. The type of music only computers and robots would be in to.

Argos catalogues

How the fuck is Santa gonna know what you want for Christmas without circling pages in the Argos catalogue and sending it to him?

Bacardi Breezers

First time I ever got pissed was on a lemon Bacardi Breezer in the park when I was 12. I was so pissed I swang for Kurtan's nan and called her a bint.

THINGS THAT USED TO EXIST THAT NO LONGER EXIST

by Kurtan Mucklowe

Things That Used To Exist That No Longer Exist

Nokia 3310

Best phone I ever had. Far more robust than the pathetic excuse for phones we got now. When your Nokia would fall on the floor it would crack the floor instead of cracking the screen and the battery life lasted for ages. I reckon even in about five thousand years' time archaeologists will dig up a Nokia and it would still have half its battery left. I feel like I never got the chance to tell that phone how much I appreciated it. Sometimes things just fade out of your life with no real reason or explanation, just like Kirk and Darren Lacey. I actually found my old Nokia in a box of stuff under my bed and turned it on. There was a message on there from Darren Lacey that said 'Do you fancy goin to Woolworths, getting some Fuse bars then going back home and watching SMTV?' After reading it I fell to my knees and just wept and wept and wept.

by Kurtan Mucklowe

Dido

You will find her face on a CD in every charity shop across the nation. Everyone thought she had the voice of a heavenly angel but I just thought she sounded like the most average teaching assistant blandly humming along as she sits marking a SATS paper. She had as much stage presence as a grain of sand on an entire beach. Her face was so plain a slice of Billy Bear ham had more charm and charisma to it. She was more forgettable than singling out a piece of gravel and then throwing it back down into the millions more gravel on your driveway. She was neither very attractive nor very ugly. She was right in the middle of the spectrum waving her boring white flag. She was blander than a bowl of runny pancake mix. I don't think Eminem even knew that Dido was in his videos. She looks like some sexless receptionist that just got lost delivering some release forms to set and ended up being in the back of shot singing along.

Dreamcast

A games console that was discontinued by SEGA. Always wanted one, never got one, glad I didn't get one. The big problem I think with Dreamcast was that it was just way ahead of its time. The world simply wasn't ready for such a marvel.

Microsoft Encarta

Like the shittiest version of Wikipedia ever, before Wikipedia existed. It had 0.0001% of the knowledge that Wikipedia has. Unless your homework was about Nelson Mandela or the pyramids you were absolutely fucked.

Things That Used to Exist *continued*

Sandpits

When was the last time you saw a sandpit? Honestly, ask yourself.

Having to speak to people's mums on the phone to get through to your friends

Having to talk to Kerry's mum every time I phoned Kerry's house was the biggest ball ache. I could be on the phone to Sue for up to 30 minutes before I got to talk to Kerry. She'd just ramble on about any old shite like 'there's a ghost in the house that keeps flushing the toilet at night' or 'that lump under my armpit's back'. Once she even gave me a live commentary about the 'You've Been Framed' episode she was watching. I'd be like 'Is Kerry there?' and she'd be like 'Kurtan…' **laugh laugh laugh** '…little baby falling over a tortoise…' **laugh laugh laugh**. It was so emotionally draining and frustrating I genuinely used to cry.

Monkeys in the PG Tips adverts wearing bowties

A crying shame I don't see these dapper little gents on our screens anymore. Not sure what monkeys had to do with tea but fuck me it was a good combination. I can imagine it was utter pandemonium on set filming them adverts. I bet they were swinging off boom mics likes trees in the jungle. Apparently they were so cheap to make cos PG Tips were literally paying the cast peanuts. It was a sad time when PG Tips dropped the monkeys from their ad campaigns and hundreds of gibbons found themselves lining up outside job centres across the UK only being able to land jobs in vivisection experiments. A lot of those monkeys are probably unrecognisable with the amount of fiddling about those lab scientists have done to them. Their best bet is to move to Jersey, live off their royalties and avoid paying tax. I wonder if any of them have PTSD and start screaming and tearing their fur out whenever someone brews up a PG Tips pyramid teabag. My biggest problem with the adverts was why did the dad monkey take so much time in wearing a freshly pressed suit and tie when he couldn't be bothered to wear a pair of shoes? What sort of business attitude does that put out to other monkeys? No wonder they're being injected with the plague in laboratories across Europe. I know monkeys' feet are a lot like human fingers but I'm sure he could have taken a pair of gloves to his local shoemaker as a template and they could have knocked something up sharpish. That's common sense but I suppose that doesn't apply to a stupid monkey.

Tony Hawk

It's pretty cool to see a young guy in his 20s doing kick flips on a halfpipe but when that same guy who is now in his 50s is STILL wearing Quiksilver shorts and STILL skating around that same halfpipe trying to impress a bunch of 12-year-olds then it's absolutely tragic. He should hang up his shorts, put on a suit and get a proper job. If not for himself then for his fucked up kids. I mean they must be fucked up if they were raised by a man who still thinks the year is 2001.

BIG MANDY'S ANGER MANAGEMENT

The Cotswold & District
Mental Wellbeing Centre

Name: Mandy Harris
Age: mind your fuckin business

Answer the following statements and add up your total score.

Circle **1** for never. Circle **2** for rarely. Circle **3** for sometimes.

Circle **4** for frequently. Circle **5** for always.

1. It's hard for me to let go of thoughts that make me angry. 1 2 3 4 (5)
2. When I become angry, I have urges to beat someone up. 1 2 3 4 (5)
3. When I become angry, I have urges to break or smash things. 1 2 3 4 (5)
4. Sometimes I get so angry I feel like a pressure-cooker, ready to explode. 1 2 3 4 (5)
5. At times, I've felt angry enough to kill. 1 2 3 4 (5)
6. I lose my temper at least once a week. 1 2 3 4 (5)
7. I get impatient when people in front of me drive at exactly the speed limit. 1 2 3 4 (5)
8. Waiting in line at the shop or waiting for other people really angers me. 1 2 3 4 (5)
9. When my neighbours are inconsiderate, it makes me angry. 1 2 3 4 (5)
10. I sometimes lie awake at night and think about the things that made me angry during the day. 1 2 3 4 (5)
11. I find myself frequently angry with certain friends or family members. 1 2 3 4 (5)
12. I get angry when people do things that they are not supposed to, like smoking in a 'no smoking section' or having more items than marked in the supermarket express checkout lane. 1 2 3 4 (5)
13. I get easily frustrated when machines/equipment do not work properly. 1 2 3 4 (5)
14. I remember for a long time people and situations that make me angry. 1 2 3 4 (5)

15. I can't tolerate incompetence. It makes me angry. 1 2 3 4 5

16. I think people try to take advantage of me, which makes me angry. 1 2 3 4 5

17. People I've trusted have often let me down, leaving me feeling angry or betrayed. 1 2 3 4 5

18. I've been so angry at times I couldn't remember things I said or did. 1 2 3 4 5

19. When someone hurts or frustrates me, I get angry and seek revenge. 1 2 3 4 5

20. I still get angry when I think of the bad things people did to me in the past. 1 2 3 4 5

TOTAL: 100

Score key:

Below **30:**

Well done! You are someone who does not find it a challenge to control their anger.

30–50:

Don't worry you are someone who gets angry as often as most people. Monitor your episodes of temper and see if you can lower your score on this test in 6 months' time.

50–60:

You have plenty of room for improvement. Reading a self-help book on anger control could be beneficial.

60–80:

You may not need professional help, but you need to work very hard on controlling your anger.

80–100:

Please seek urgent professional help.

please turn the page

Further Questions:

1) Have you been physically violent in the past? If yes, please give incidents, against whom, etc.

Yeah of course but not without darn good reason.

2) Do you have any addictions, such as alcohol, nicotine, drugs? If yes, please give details.

Hannah Spearritt is a type of drug I suppose.

3) How do you know when you're angry?

When I black out and wake up to me punching someone/something.

4) What do you experience in your body when you're angry?

Tingling in my fists when punching things.

5) Who were your role models for expressing anger?

My dad. If there was something wrong like the toaster for example he'd punch it until it started working again.

6) What was the effect of your anger within your family?

Less Christmas cards.

7) What is it about your anger that you fear the most?

The stalking side because I can and will love someone to death.

8) What is it about your anger that you most appreciate and respect?

Sometimes when I'm really angry i can throw a car engine over 5 metres which i think is actually quite impressive if you look at the stats of it. I'm also quite proud of the fact I can cause maximum agony without technically causing death.

9) After expressing your anger, what is the first thing you usually do?

Check to see what the weathers doin on my phone. Don't know why, just a habit I suppose.

10) Can you think back to a time when you started becoming angry?

When I was 4 years old I got run over by a dodgem and my head ain't been the same since. I've seen some doctors who reckon it's something to do with them little sparks at the top of the dodgems that's just scrambled my neurons and ever since I've had a problem with processing my emotional responses to things. I often mix love with hate and sympathy with anger, for example a few years back a little disabled chap came to the door selling cupcakes and I got so overwhelmed with emotion listening to his story I ended up bashing his head into the doorframe.

11) Does your anger push your loved ones away?

Yes, I ended up sending seventy thousand hate-filled tweets to Hannah Spearritt via Twitter and she blocked me. Im also banned by the police from climbing into her loft and waiting there for hours which is annoying cos I really enjoyed that. Used to keep myself warm with old rugs and curtains.

12) Is there anyone specifically that makes you more angry than others?

Kurtan. No one should look that ugly and be able to get away with it.

13) Any other things that have made you angry recently?

Fish tank filters.

LEN'S SPOOKY TALES

by Len Clifton

Len's Spooky Tales

Me ancestors have inhabited this village since the dawn of time and there ain't nothin bout this place I don't know. Records of the village start as far back as the Doomsday Book where me great ancestor Len VIII even got a mention as a 'peasant who had something to say about everyone and everything' – so much so that in 1085 his tongue was cut out in front of the Earl of Gloucester for being an idle gossip. What people don't know is that ancient ley lines run underneath the village. The very same lines than run from Stonehenge and all the way to the pyramids in Egypt. Some say that's the reason for the odd goings on around this place. Others say it's the hapless county council. Personally I think it's a bit of both. I have decided to gather together the famous myths and legends of the village that I was told when I was a youngen which were passed down to me through the generations. So hold on to yer crucifixes and don't turn out the lights…

The Vanishing Tour Guide

This ghostly tale I've heard from a few people over the recent years and it will send shivers down yer spine. Our village being nestled deep in the soft bosom of the Cotswold countryside is a magnet for tourists from all over the globe. There have been many a tale of Japanese tourists being greeted off the coach in the market place by a gentleman wearing a tall stovepipe hat with a wide brim who shouts in an authoritative manner, 'This way, this way!' The Japanese tourists follow him for up to 12 miles, deep into the countryside, where the tour guide is known to drop to his knees, put his head in his hands and say, 'Shit, I don't know where the fuck we are,' before vanishing into thin air. The chap in the top hat fits the description of a local tour guide known by the name of Ernie Garlick whose trademark was wearing a tall stovepipe top hat with a wide brim. Tragically Ernie took his own life in 1987 when he read a cruel review of one of his tours in *Cotswold Life* magazine. The poor fella just weren't naturally blessed with the directional skills

needed of a tour guide and was even known to get lost in his very own street. He suffered from a disorder called topographical agnosia which causes a person to have absolutely zero sense of direction. It's a comfort, however, to know that Ernie is still doing what he loves beyond the grave and guiding tourists into the arse end of nowhere. God bless yer Ernie, yer half-wit…

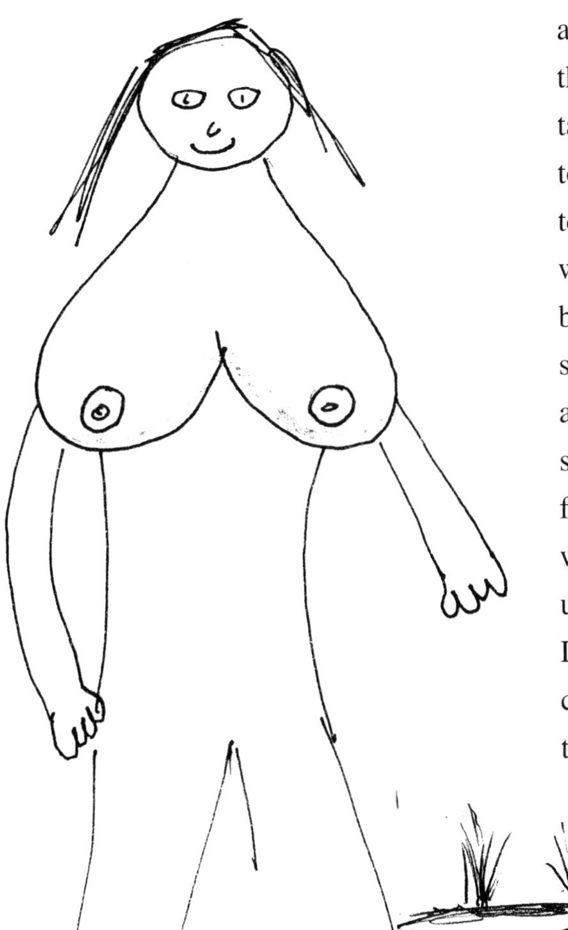

The Big-Breasted Nymph

This legend has been passed on through countless generations and is one that has both inspired and terrified many a young chap. The story goes that our very own village pond is home to a nymph – a beautiful maiden blessed with the biggest pair of breasts you'll ever see. She is known to rise up out the water in all her beauty and coax many an angler across the pond to grab a good handful before getting tangled up in the pond weed and succumbing to a watery death. The only angler that lived to tell the tale was a chap called Roger Gardner, who recalled during a day's fishing on the pond back in the 1950s that the beautiful maiden suddenly appeared out the water in a green mist and swung her jugs in a hypnotic fashion. Roger stayed on the bankside as he had a preference for small tits but his mate Dave trudged into the water, enchanted, before sinking to the bottom under the weight of his large erected rod. Poor Dave found himself, like many of his fish, caught hook, line and sinker. But you know how the old sayin goes, 'karma's a bitch'.

Len's Spooky Tales *continued*

The Beast of Purley Road

A 'beast' is known to wreak havoc among the recycling bins in Purley Road. Most of the activity happens to occur the night before bin day, when all the bins are lined up on the pavements outside ready for collection from the bin men the following morning. On one occasion, a resident noticed bite marks in an empty tin of chopped tomatoes and one person claimed to have seen the beast eat an entire bird table before retreating back into the darkness. The beast is easily spooked and very few sightings have actually been recounted. Rumours are rife as to what form the beast takes. Some say it's an escaped panther from Cotswold Wildlife Park, others say it's an Alsatian-sized hedgehog. But just for the record it's definitely not me. OK?

The Time Slip

Legend has it that on certain days of the year the footpath behind the Keepers is known to see its walkers enter a different dimension of time, known as a 'time slip'. In 1969 a village resident called Harry Greaves was walking home down the footpath after a daytime session at the Keepers and suddenly noticed that the ground he was walking on looked unfamiliar. He looked to his left and saw a floating 'spaceship-like' building where the pharmacy was normally located. A man ran towards him, completely naked, screaming, 'Robots have taken over the world!' Harry asked him what year it was and the man shook him and replied, 'ARE YOU CRAZY?! IT'S THE YEAR 2022 OF COURSE!' Then, before Harry knew it, the time slip was over and he was back in the year 1969. Harry said it had nothing to do with the 3 tabs of LSD he took while in the Keepers that day and insisted he would never forget the face of the man he saw. 'He had tiny little eyes, and was small in stature'. It wasn't until years later when Harry was watching a programme called 'New Faces' and a very young, undiscovered Jim Davidson stepped up to the mic to crack some jokes. Harry's heart almost stopped, he pointed at the television and let out a scream. 'What's wrong?' asked his wife. 'That's the man I saw in the time slip!' Work that one out then…

by Len Clifton

The Fox Twins

Local legend has it that two beastly brothers inhabit the woods on the outskirts of the village. Over the years dog walkers have reported seeing two 'half-men, half-fox-like' creatures running around on all fours devouring rotting animal carcasses. No one knows the origin of the twins. Some say they were the product of an 'experiment gone wrong' by a mad scientist in the 1940s who was employed by the Ministry of Defence to come up with the ultimate human killing machine. Others say they were the result of some dirty bastard who shagged a fox and I know what yer thinking…I AIN'T EVER DONE IT WITH A FOX! OK?

The Rectory Demon

According to legend, this village is so damned that the Pope refuses to fly over it as it's reputed to be one of the seven gates to hell. This is backed up with a story of a demon known to terrorise the occupants of the rectory over the last few centuries. In the 19th century alone over fourteen hundred vicars moved in and moved out of the rectory claiming to have been victims of demonic possessions. Many accounts from the vicars told of the demon possessing them during sermons to shout vile personal insults to the congregation. One account told that during a particular sermon in 1892 Reverend John Foster pointed at an elderly woman sat on a first-row pew and said, 'The last time I saw something like you, I flushed it down the toilet.' One vicar described how he was so possessed during an evening choir practice that he pulled down his trousers and mooned at the organist. An excavation in the 1920s of the grounds of the rectory discovered evidence of satanic worship. Historians have said that one of the practices of these devil worshippers was to pull down their pants and moony at the cross. Spooky or what??

THE BIG HOUSE
BOOM

KERRY AND KURTAN'S INTERVIEW IN THE *GLOUCESTERSHIRE ECHO*

The Gloucestershire Echo

75p

21st June 2018

Stars of BBC documentary 'This Country' interview

by Josh Wright

Hi Kerry and Kurtan. You recently appeared in the BBC3 documentary 'This Country', which aired earlier this year and is about young people living in modern day rural Britain. What was it like having your every move documented by the crew?

Kerry: It was annoying cos they were just always there hangin around and asking for plug sockets to charge their camera batteries. They once unplugged the Sky box which erased everything we recorded on Sky planner since 2015...

Kurtan: There was 34 hours worth of 'The One Show' just wiped off the face of the earth.

Kerry: And they tramped mud up all the stairs as well, which my mum was not happy about, despite me telling them on numerous occasions to take their shoes off.

Kurtan: They never replaced any teabags either...

Do you feel the documentary was a fair representation of you?

Kerry: No. They made me look like a buffoon. What you need to understand is that I have a large range of different skills which I was doing on a day-to-day basis but they just cut it all from the show. For example, me and Kurtan started a club in the village called Jackass Club which is basically us doing unbelievably mad stunts to make people laugh...

continued on p4

14 day weather forecast on page 22

Kerry and Kurtan in the village square

...continued from p3 I've been doing it since I was at school...just started off doing small things like drinking Tipp-Ex, eating Pritt Stick, stapling my ear to my neck, that sort of thing...then when the cameras were here I was doing bigger stuff like caning it off roofs, falling through skylights, getting up on the bus shelter and trying to jump on top on the bus...I even went on the monkey bars while Levi shot at me with his Grandad's pellet rifle...but did they show it?...Did they f***.

Kurtan: Yeah...and there was a scene where I travelled to Stroud to meet my dog's parents...but I can understand why they edited that out cos nothing really happened...

Kerry: Kurtan's convinced he was CGI'd in some of his scenes as well...

Kurtan: Yeah I was...Cos firstly I don't remember doing or saying half those things and secondly my voice is completely different in real life. They dubbed over me with who my Nan thinks is Ioan Gruffudd from *Hornblower*...and I looked him up and he does actually do a lot of voiceover work.

Kerry: And tell him about the hovering as well...

Kurtan: If you look carefully in every scene I'm in, my trainers are hovering 3 inches off the ground.

...continued on p5

Horoscopes on page 24

...continued from p4

Further proof I was merely a computer-generated image.

Do you watch documentaries yourself?

Kurtan: I watched a documentary on how they made Wallace and Gromit. Apparently they made Gromit's character miserable because it would have taken them 10 years to animate Gromit wagging his tail in every scene.

What have you learned from the experience?

Kerry: Don't trust anyone... especially Beardy Graham from the BBC. Cos when he comes to you offering a chance to do a documentary about your life he's actually gonna pull your pants down in front of an entire nation...

Kurtan: But it got me thinking about the bigger picture...If shows like this are manipulated then what else has the public been fooled into thinking is true? Like is Trump really President of America or is he actually a Russian spy?

Kerry: Yeah, and are the Chuckle Brothers really brothers or are they actually father and son?

How have people responded to the documentary?

Kerry: People were quite harsh about us.

Kurtan: Yeah, especially with the way we look.

Kerry: Someone on Twitter wrote 'Kurtan from "This Country" is so thin he wears a Hula Hoop for a belt'.

Kurtan: Yeah...and just for the record, I don't wear a hula hoop for a belt. I wear a belt for a belt.

Would you do another series of 'This Country' if the BBC asked you?

Kerry: Yes.

Kurtan: Yes. Definitely.

Free Ads

Kids scooters x 2. one blue, one pink. suit 5 - 8 year olds. £25 for the pair. Tel 07414 236987

Assorted plant pots - 48 plastic seedling pots, 24 medium plastic pots, 4 large terracotta patio pots. £30. greenfingers21@gmail.com

Haynes manuals - Astra Mk4, Mondeo 1997-2000, Citroen C4 diesel 2012-2015, Mini One 1.6, Citroen Xantia 2.0L Mk2 - £4 each. Tel. 07421 443213.

Angling Times Magazines - approx 200 copies in binders. Mostly from 1992-1998. £50 or £1 each. Telephone. 07973 503112

Table and six dining chairs. Bought from Argos last year. £40. buyer to collect. diane.rogers62@hotmail.com

Box of CDs - approx 80. mostly pop but some rock. £35 07975 125251

Closing Note

We hope you enjoyed this special edition of the Parish Newsletter. Normally, here you would find a long list of names of people we would like to thank for their help in making the newsletter, but the only people we want to thank is ourselves. We have been incredible on this journey and we can't thank ourselves enough for that. So instead we would like to acknowledge the people we would NOT like to thank.

We would NOT like to thank:

- Kirsty Taylor, for breaking Kurtan's heart and being an utter gutter skunk.
- Arthur, for keeping us sat in his living room for 1 hour 45 minutes, showing us old pictures of him flying his model planes. Neither was it useful nor at all relevant to ANYTHING other than his own selfish satisfaction.
- Kerry's mum, for constantly kicking us out of the house when we were trying to work, so we had to use the Wendy house in the park as an office.
- Mrs Wix, for not letting us steal the pens we needed to write this newsletter.
- June, for being such a miserable old boot bag and getting her weird bald son to put us under citizen's arrest for simply picking bunches of flowers from her garden and selling them.

If you were offended by any of the contents in this newsletter please post your complaints to:
PO BOX GET STUFFED,
FUCK YOU STREET,
ISLE OF FUCK OFF,
FU.CK OFF

Cheers,

KERRY MUCKLOWE

Kurtan Mucklowe

In memory of Michael Sleggs 1985-2019

"Thank the Lord for Slugs"

big-breasted nymph
seen here – allegedly

Big Mundy's
place
(psycho)

Found a dead
badger here